SELF-MASTERY
THROUGH
SELF-HYPNOSIS

Dr. Roger Bernhardt and David Martin

SELF-MASTERY
THROUGH
SELF-HYPNOSIS

The Bobbs-Merrill Company, Inc.
INDIANAPOLIS / NEW YORK

Published by The Bobbs-Merrill Company, Inc.
Indianapolis   New York

Designed by Ingrid Beckman
Manufactured in the United States of America

First printing

Library of Congress Cataloging in Publication Data

Bernhardt, Roger, 1915-
    Self-mastery through self-hypnosis.

    1. Autogenic training. 2. Success. I. Martin,
David, 1931-   joint author. II. Title.
RC499.A8B38   158'.1   77-76876
ISBN 0-672-52058-3

Acknowledgments

Above all, to my patients: while none was treated for purposes of this writing and all who are mentioned are, we trust, well disguised, they are clearly the *sine qua non* of this work, to whom we express heartfelt gratitude.

Two instructors: my psychoanalytic mentor, the late, great Edmund Bergler, M.D., is the main source of any in-depth insights into the human mind that may underlie this effort. Herbert Spiegel, M.D., Clinical Professor of Psychiatry at Columbia University College of Physicians and Surgeons, quoted in these pages for specific contributions, was a fountain of information on hypnosis.

Four close partners: Hubert Simon, whose extraordinary brain is matched only by the greatness of his heart; Jay Sutherland, Dr. Ruby Kaplan and Edmund Carmody were lavish in their counsel and support.

Finally, my full gratitude goes to cherished family allies who constantly sprang to the rescue with a touch of wisdom or a sign of caring.

—R.B.

I wish to express my gratitude to Marj, John and Cynthia for their patience, their understanding, their sufferance, and, in circumstances often less than serene as this book was being wrestled into submission, their unflagging if unwarranted good cheer. I would also like to acknowledge a special debt, incalculable as it is unpayable, to my mother and father for all that went into the earlier years; only they know how much.

—D.M.

We feel a special gratitude to our editor, Diane Giddis. Her expertise, patience and encouragement were invaluable.

—R.B. and D.M.

Contents

SELF-MASTERY
THROUGH
SELF-HYPNOSIS

CHAPTER 1

=====

Can I Be Hypnotized?

If you have ever "lost" yourself reading a book, listening to music, or watching a play or a movie—you've been hypnotized.

If your mind has ever wandered and you've forgotten for a moment where you were or failed to hear someone speak your name—you've been hypnotized.

If you've ever become so absorbed in a task that you lose all track of time—you've been hypnotized.

If you've every fallen in love and been rendered blind to the charms of others—you've been hypnotized.

If you've ever felt "transported" in prayer—you've been hypnotized.

As you can see, virtually everyone has been hypnotized, or, more accurately, has hypnotized himself; for all hypnosis, whether accomplished with the aid of a hypnotist or not, is self-hypnosis. The experience may have been so spontaneous that you were not even aware it was happening, as in the situations described above, or it may have been an intentional, self-started and self-controlled exercise leading to the achievement of a desired goal. Teaching you exactly how to employ self-hypnosis for a specific purpose is the aim of this book.

You may well wonder, "Can I hypnotize myself?" Chances are you've seen hypnosis performed or at least read about it and acknowledged that such a thing as hypnosis may possibly exist—for others. "But how about me?" Let's look at the odds.

Experts in the field, M.D.'s and Ph.D.'s who are devoting their professional lives to the practice and study of hypnosis, estimate that from 80 to 90 percent of the population can be hypnotized. It is my belief that anyone who is not neurologically impaired, retarded or psychotic can benefit from self-hypnosis. If you suffer none of these afflictions, the odds are overwhelmingly in your favor that you can hypnotize yourself. However, I find there are two important prerequisites to being hypnotized: (1) a sincere desire and (2) an open mind.

An open mind does not preclude a healthy skepticism. A case in point: myself. Throughout my schooling and for years as a practicing psychoanalyst, I considered hypnosis unimportant; it just wasn't done in my academic and professional circles. But once exposed to its considerable potentials (I check my inclination to say "limitless potentials"), I became a convert, and rarely does a more devout advocate of a cause exist than a convert to it. So I emphasize: If you do not at this point already possess a hard conviction that you probably can hypnotize yourself, keep your mind open to the *possibility* that you can, and be willing to learn.

Of course, even if you agree that you may be hypnotizable, you may still ask why you should hypnotize yourself: "What will hypnosis do for me?" I find it difficult to be conservative in assessing the benefits of hypnosis. Others in the field are equally enthusiastic. The English scientist J. B. S. Haldane has written: "Anyone who has seen even a single example of the power of hypnotism and suggestion must realize that the face of the world and the possibilities of existence will be totally altered when we can control their effects and standardize their application, as has been possible, for example, with drugs which were once regarded as equally magical."

That's a pretty strong statement, but it is indicative of the respect many knowledgeable men of science hold for the potential applications of hypnosis.

What hypnosis can do for you depends largely on what you want it to do. For hypnosis is goal-directed. You practice the hypnotic exercise not as an end in itself—though in itself it is pleasurable—but as a means of effecting a change in yourself. The change may involve a habit you wish to break; you may want to quit smoking, to cut down on drinking, to lose weight. You may hope to conquer a fear, such as the fear of flying. You may yearn to diminish the pain of headache, arthritis, dentistry, childbirth. You may desire to overcome insomnia, chronic fatigue, nervousness, depression. You may long to become more assertive and self-confident in your own abilities. All these and more are attainable through self-hypnosis.

Even the individual who claims not to have a habit he wants to break, a fear or phobia he wants to lose, or an attitude that needs changing can gain from practicing self-hypnosis. For is there anyone who would not benefit from a simple, brief relaxation exercise that relieves tension and curbs anxiety?

Many techniques exist for achieving self-hypnosis. The one you will learn in this book is my favorite, the one I teach my patients. It is swift and simple and can be employed almost anywhere—at the office, on the subway, in the classroom, in your easy chair. Once you master it, you can enter and emerge from the self-hypnotic exercise in about thirty seconds, and without revealing to anyone around you that you're up to anything.

In the coming chapters I will attempt to shed light on what hypnosis really is and to chip away at the myths that stubbornly adhere to the concept. Although we will explore the phenomenon and try to expand your understanding of it, my main objective is empirical: to teach you how to use the tool of self-hypnosis to help yourself. If you learn a little more about its history and its workings, so much the better, but we will be concerned not so much with why it works as with how you can put it to work for you. You don't know why aspirin cures your headache (neither does your doctor, for that matter); all you care about is that the pain is gone. Such is the case with hypnosis.

Impressive as the results of hypnotic therapy are, a cautionary word should be sounded: it is not a miraculous cure-all. Hypnosis will accomplish nothing that other therapeutic approaches will not accomplish; it will simply do it faster. When a patient comes to me for analysis, he often brings with him ancillary problems which, while not disabling, are bothersome. Often they respond quite readily to hypnotherapy. Why spend our time and his money on complaints that self-hypnosis can quickly clear up?

But if hypnosis simply does faster what other forms of therapy can do, it does a great deal more than self-help programs alone. Based on the best of intentions, self-help plans just don't do the trick for many people. We all know what road is paved with good intentions, and it's not of yellow brick. Most of us need a boost, a shot of psychic adrenalin to move us off our lassitude. We can read countless self-help books that exhort us to think sunny thoughts, to like ourselves, to calm down, pep up, or relax, to improve in every way—but that doesn't seem to be enough.

Hypnosis provides a little something extra. Not only does it create a climate of tranquillity and repose; not only does it allow us to focus our concentration creatively; most important, it brings us to an elevated state of consciousness or awareness, a sort of shifting of psychic gears onto a higher plane. This raised state of awareness permits a *linkage* with the unconscious, not the sleeplike state of unconsciousness itself that is all too often in the public mind associated with hypnosis. When a person telephones to Australia, he's not in Australia but in communication with Australia. When you practice hypnosis, you're not unconscious, but you are in touch with your unconscious mind. And that makes all the difference between hypnosis and other approaches to self-improvement.

Although hypnotizability itself cannot be predicted with accuracy, clinical experience and laboratory experiments at such institutions as Harvard and Stanford suggest that the individuals most susceptible to hypnosis tend to share certain qualities. As stated earlier, virtually everyone can benefit from hypnosis. Still, if you possess most of these qualities, studies indicate that you may be more readily and easily hypnotizable than those who do not.

Here, then, are some of the criteria of hypnotizability:

1. *Motivation.* At the top of the list comes motivation. If you don't want to be hypnotized, you won't be—and you probably wouldn't be reading this book, either. If you want strongly enough to change something, chances are good that you can hypnotize yourself into doing so. But such motivation must come from inside; you yourself must sincerely desire to change, and not because others think you should or because it's the fashion.

Let me cite an example. A woman came to see me to be hypnotized for smoking. I asked her why.

"Because it bothers my husband, and he wants me to stop," she replied.

"What about you?" I asked.

"It really doesn't bother me," she said. "I smoke a pack a day, but I don't think it's hurting me. I'm not worried about cancer or emphysema or anything like that."

My response was, "Your motivation seems to be to do what others want you to do, not what you want to do yourself."

"Exactly," she agreed. "That's the way I was brought up."

This woman was in analysis with me, so I told her, "Let's postpone the hypnosis until you get interested in doing it because *you* want to."

2. *Optimism.* If you take a continuum of hypnotizability from low to high, the people at the high end tend not to be skeptics. This does not mean that if you are skeptical now you can't hypnotize yourself. But it is hoped that by the time you finish this book your skepticism will have relaxed somewhat, enabling you to more easily experience hypnosis. The most hypnotizable people, it has been found, are likely to have a hopeful, optimistic attitude toward life. For them, the bottle is not half-empty but half-full.

3. *Advocacy.* The person who finds hypnosis most accessible tends to be an advocate. This is an extension of the buoyancy, trust and hope that his optimism reflects. Whether it be something new in medicine, politics, art, or whatever piques his interest, he enthusiastically wants to spread the word. His opposite is the person who is very cognitive, very

scientific in his appraisal; this individual demands evidence, wants to read half a dozen books, and explores the subject thoroughly before he commits himself. Not that this cerebral attitude is wrong; it simply means that to get results, such a reality-oriented individual will have to stay with hypnosis longer.

4. *Concentration.* An important characteristic of the state of hypnosis is a condition of heightened concentration. Although hypnosis deepens concentration, the very ability to concentrate in the first place is necessary to achieve the state. The more distractible a person is, the more he will report, when he attempts to hypnotize himself or to be hypnotized by another, "Well, I'm just aware of everything going on around me, and my mind wanders to how I'm getting along with my wife and the bills and this and that." He too has to use the method more often to gain benefit.

On the other hand, most people are capable of deep concentration, at least some of the time. Go into a room where someone is reading a book and call his name—you get no response. He's concentrating so hard that he simply doesn't hear you. I don't find evidence that there's any difference between such a state of intense concentration and self-hypnosis itself.

5. *Receptivity.* Many people are frightened of being hypnotized, lest they submerge themselves in another's will. This might be called the Svengali syndrome: the mysterious stranger with black cloak and flinty eye snatching the soul of a nubile maid as he bends her will to conform to his nefarious wishes. In actuality, a highly hypnotizable person is of normal or superior intelligence and is possessed of a hard core of beliefs and fixed attitudes that are basic to his life. An example of such a person is one with a fairly disciplined religious upbringing who is receptive to new ideas. He's not gullible; he's susceptible to reasonable suggestions.

Some individuals, of course, are more receptive than others. Take, for example, a man who has come to me for psychoanalysis. Married just four months ago, he finds he is "irrationally jealous" if his wife merely glances around a room where other men are present. Although he came for analysis, I think this man may be a favorable subject for hypnosis, too. What are my grounds for this guess? He comes with an openness, a real "I know you're going to help me" attitude. Having read a book in which the writer praises me, he says he knows I'm going to help him solve his problems.

Your suggestibility, your ability to welcome new ideas, is one of the determinants of how easily you can be hypnotized. On a scale of zero to five (zero being people who cannot be hypnotized) the bulk of the population will fall in the middle, let's say in the area of two and three.

Take solace, however, if the degree of your susceptibility to hypnosis doesn't qualify you for a five rating. You may have to repeat hypnosis more frequently if you're a two or a three, but there are disadvantages as well as advantages to being on the upper end of the scale. I'm thinking of a man who came to me with an ache in his groin which he attributed to a fall he'd experienced a year before. I sent him to a urologist friend who found no physiological or organic basis for this ache. So, following the usual induction, I suggested to him that when he emerged he would find himself relieved of discomfort. Further, by the time he awoke the following morning the ache would be completely gone. And that's just the way it turned out. He's a "high," rating between a four and a five. Yet when you talk with this man, you sense that suggestibility can be overdone. For years he was a very willing victim to his father's ordering him about, so much so that he scarcely had a life of his own. He felt himself to be a puppet; whenever his father snapped his fingers, he jumped. (Psychoanalysis was indicated to reduce the impressionable child in this able, bright man.)

A similar story is told of a highly accomplished surgeon here in New York City, a five so suggestible that he became the target of people who wanted to borrow money or get contributions. He was well-to-do, and he found that before he knew it he'd be writing large checks for organizations he wasn't interested in. When asked, he just couldn't say no. He was finally advised to require a countersignature on his checks. Thereafter, on writing a check, he'd hand it to the requesting person and say, "Oh, by the way, another signature is required for this—see my lawyer."

So if, like most people, you're a two or a three in susceptibility, be content if the benefits of self-hypnosis don't come in a day; there are compensations.

6. *Imagination.* For nearly two decades scientists at the Laboratory of Hypnosis Research of the Department of Psychology at Stanford University have been conducting studies of the differences in hypnotizability among individuals. It is a project supported by the National Institute of Mental Health and the Air Force Office of Scientific Research, organizations not inclined to fund frivolous endeavors. Reporting on this research, Dr. Josephine R. Hilgard, clinical professor of psychiatry at Stanford, has written:

"We have evidence that those who, for one reason or another, kept alive the imaginative involvements of childhood were the ones who retained their hypnotizability. . . . The theory is that the *capacity* for imaginative and adventurous involvement, originating early in life, has been kept alive and functional through continuous use. Among the college students, the involvements that were found to be related to hypnosis included reading, drama, creativity, childhood imagination, religion, sensory stimulation, and adventurousness. [The hynotizable person is] capable of deep involvement in one or more imaginative-feeling areas of experience— reading a novel, listening to music, having an aesthetic experience of nature, or engaging in absorbing adventures of body or mind."

Dr. Hilgard found humanities majors most susceptible to hypnosis, social science majors next, and science and engineering students least hypnotizable.

Experience and research by other workers in the field tend to confirm the Stanford findings. Dr. Lewis R. Wolberg, an authority on the subject for forty years and currently Clinical Professor of Psychiatry at New York University Medical School, has written:

"Individuals who relish sensory experiences, or who are able to project themselves into roles, like actors, show a greater aptitude for hypnosis than others. In Dr. Hilgard's laboratory, individuals who had imaginary companions in childhood, who read a great deal, and who had a capacity for immersing themselves in adventure or nature were most susceptible. I have found that suspicious, withdrawn, and hostile people tend to resist hypnosis."

Few individuals will rank high in all the criteria enumerated above: motivation, optimism, advocacy, concentration, receptivity and imagination; nor need you show strength in every area. What you lack in one category you can compensate for in another.

And now, having set forth these criteria, I would like to insert a qualifier. An enormous amount of research in hypnosis remains to be done. Only in recent years have the academic and medical communities accepted the subject as one worthy of serious inquiry. Although evidence to date indicates that possessing these criteria contributes to hypnotizability, there is simply no certain means of predicting who can and who cannot be hypnotized. As put by Ernest R. Hilgard (husband of the aforementioned Dr. Josephine R. Hilgard), professor of psychology and Director of the Laboratory of Hypnosis Research at Stanford:

"It can be said with confidence that there is no diagnostic category that precludes hypnotic susceptibility; correspondingly there is none that guarantees it. At least two studies (including our own) are in agreement that normal subjects are more hypnotizable than those that border on the neurotic or are frankly neurotic. This should help correct the public image that being susceptible to hypnosis is a sign of weakness or instability."

I had a patient, a professor from Boston, head of his department. He'd made rapid and effective progress in analysis, then returned because of some work problems of a minor sort he thought hypnosis might help. This man has all the criteria of a person of high susceptibility: he is trusting, suspends judgment, tends to be an advocate of a point of view or cause, tends to live in the present, possesses a good memory, has an ability to concentrate well, is hospitable to new ideas, but still has a hard core of beliefs of his own. Yet he was a hard-line zero in every point of a test I gave him for hypnotizability. This is why I ultimately ride with the view that we know a person is hypnotizable *after* he's been hypnotized.

The Boston professor was a member of the small minority in the population who probably cannot experience hypnosis (although even such an inability can be transitory). You the reader, however, very probably are among the great majority of people who can hypnotize themselves. Assume you are innocent of inability until proved otherwise. My advice:

1. Follow the hypnotic induction procedure detailed in later chapters, confident that you have hypnotized yourself up to your ability at that time.

2. Give yourself whatever implants for change or improvement you wish.

3. Repeat the procedure religiously, knowing that each experience will contribute toward cumulative benefit.

Many practitioners, myself included, regard self-hypnosis as a cognitive skill that can be both learned and sharpened. If at first you don't hypnotize, try tomorrow and tomorrow's tomorrow and the tomorrow after that. I am convinced that with determination and perseverance, nine out of ten of the readers of this book can learn to hypnotize themselves, using the fastest and simplest technique I know.

There is, however, one simple experiment that can tell you whether you are probably capable of being hypnotized, and also give a very rough idea of your level of susceptibility to hypnosis. It's called the Eye-Roll test and takes just a few seconds.

Dr. Herbert Spiegel, clinical professor of psychiatry at Columbia University's College of Physicians and Surgeons, examined 2,000 subjects in order to test the thesis that individuals who are most hypnotizable have the capacity to roll their eyes upward in their heads. Conversely, persons who are not hypnotizable cannot direct their gaze upward.

"It is generally observed," Dr. Spiegel wrote, "that when a person wants to concentrate intensely without interference, one postural stance is to look upward. Sometimes this is followed by eye closure and is consistent with the need to reduce peripheral awareness to facilitate focal attention. The Eye-Roll test is an extension of this. . . . In about 75% of the 2,000 consecutive cases, a five-second examination predicted hypnotic trance capacity."

Add to the above results Spiegel's further finding: 99 percent of the hypnotizable subjects showed a positive eye-roll. This ability to send one's eyes up into the head is considered by some workers to be a neurological phenomenon that happens with certain people and doesn't with others. If the person just stares straight ahead, and some people will, we can be virtually sure that this person is not hypnotizable.

Here's how to perform the test on yourself:

1. Keep your head steady and look straight ahead.

2. Without moving your head, look upward with your eyes toward your eyebrows, then higher, toward the top of your head.

3. With your eyes held in this upward gaze, slowly close your eyelids.

4. Open your eyelids and let your eyes return to normal focus.

You can judge for yourself whether your eyes turn upward during the test: if you see the ceiling, the eye-roll works, and you probably can hypnotize yourself. If, in spite of your efforts, you continue to view the wall or whatever is directly in front of you at eye level, it isn't working. The likelihood then is that you will not experience the raised state of self-hypnosis, although you can still benefit from practicing the exercise. Just how will be explained later.

CHAPTER 2

Facts and Fables About Hypnosis

"All sciences alike have descended from magic and superstition, but none has been so slow as hypnosis in shaking off the evil association of its origin."

So wrote Clark L. Hull, a pioneer in attempting to legitimize hypnosis, four decades ago. And although significant inroads have been made in scientific circles in the intervening years—today, in this country alone, some 15,000 doctors, dentists and psychologists are qualified practitioners—the lay public remains uninformed and misinformed. In this chapter we will try to peel fiction from fact and remove the obstacles that may have kept you from enjoying the benefits of hypnosis until now.

The very word itself gets us off on the wrong mental foot, to perform a neat metaphorical trick. The word "hypnotism" (I find the synonymous word "hypnosis" more congenial) was coined little more than a century ago by a Scottish physician, James Braid. Unfortunately, it is derived from the Greek word *hypnos*, "to put to sleep." Later in life, as Dr. Braid delved deeper into the nature of the phenomenon, he tried to supplant the word "hypnotism" with the more accurately descriptive *mono ideism*, "one thought." But the former had already planted itself so firmly in popular usage that it has stuck till this day.

To be sure, subsequent practitioners of the technique are

hardly helpful in differentiating hypnosis from sleep when they speak of the "hypnotic trance," of entering "a deep, sound, refreshing sleep," and of "waking up." Nevertheless, let us concern ourselves here with aspects of the experience itself, not with the word used to describe it.

Even though it is entered into in a state of relaxation, hypnosis is actually the opposite of sleep. Unlike sleep, during which we relinquish contact with the world around us, hypnosis is a state of sharpened awareness and focused concentration in which our receptivity to suggestions is heightened.

Yet through the years myths feed on and regenerate themselves through repetition, compounding the errors resulting from knowledge dimly perceived and inadequately interpreted. Thus the persistent image of the hypnotist: a demon with electrically charged fingers firing bolts of power at helpless subjects, much like Michelangelo's God bestowing the spark of life on Adam.

If I may be allowed a moment of confession: I shared such misconceptions long into my adult and professional life. I had been in the field of emotional health for more than twenty years, fifteen of them as a psychoanalyst, before I accepted hypnosis as a valid form of therapy. Why did it take me so long? There are several reasons.

First, when one is reared a Freudian, it's almost as if there is only one true church and all the others are havens for sinners. Freud had explored hypnosis and then given it up; it just didn't solve the problems he wanted to solve. I find this ironic, since part of the reason I've adopted hypnosis is that analysis faltered on some problems that hypnotherapy has quite efficiently solved.

There's another point regarding Freud and hypnotherapy: in psychoanalysis one never comes in contact with the patient. As a psychoanalyst I never touch a patient. In hypnosis it's approved routinely; *e.g.,* in testing for hypnotizability, there is a stroking of the finger, a touching of the arm. This is not only part of the technique, it's even considered helpful—the laying on of hands.

Then there was the persistent belief that hypnotherapy was

merely a symptom swapper, that if it cleared up one symptom, a different symptom would appear. Get rid of a headache and you get a toothache. This fear, that one simply cures a symptom only to have something perhaps worse rear up, is not based on fact.

The bias appears to be a product of the times. In the late 1800s, the science of physics was in the forefront. Consider hydraulics. We have closed systems: push this lever down and that one comes up. Within that context, the human being was understandably cast into that model. Scientists assumed that what was true of a mechanical contrivance must be true of the human mechanism. Later researchers found that the human being is not such a closed system. But the bias persisted.

Furthermore, those of us who studied psychoanalysis and clinical psychology in the 1950s learned little about hypnosis—partly because of the reasons I've mentioned, partly because we in training shared the low professional opinion of hypnosis as a kind of trick that belongs on the stage. There was even skepticism that there *was* such a thing as hypnosis. That anyone would seriously use "hocus-pocus" for curative purposes, for therapeutic work, simply was not part of the thinking of that era.

Yet another reason I stayed aloof from hypnosis for so long, one that is common among psychoanalysts (and laymen), was the belief that the hypnotist assumes a "power position" in relation to the subject. The strict Freudians remained in the background, just listening and letting the patient work his way out of his neurosis. Hypnosis seemed to take the reverse of that position. Many of us assumed that a hypnotherapist must have a "Svengali" power over the patient.

Later, of course, I discovered that this is not the case at all, that while in the initial period a hypnotherapist may assume a positive role, it's the patient who hypnotizes himself, and certainly thereafter it's strictly self-hypnosis all the way.

So all of the above served to keep this psychoanalyst distant from this method until recent years. Yet, in my practice I was continually encountering certain difficulties that were not being answered swiftly by analysis. People with deep problems would have adjunctive ones, such as smoking. They had friends dying of cancer and emphysema and feared a similar fate. There was a need to get rid of such problems fast.

Analysis doesn't work fast. Analysis is a slow, gradual process of self-exploration. When I learned that hypnotherapy was a method that in a very short time, in a single session in some cases, could enable one to stop smoking, and that this was only one of several habits or problems that could be radically changed, if not eradicated, I became intrigued with the possibilities of the method.

I met Dr. Lewis R. Wolberg when he gave a lecture at a meeting of the New York Society for Clinical Psychologists, and I was impressed. Here was a highly regarded psychiatrist-psychoanalyst who had written a volume on hypnosis. He was receiving patients sent by other analysts who were bumping against problems they weren't solving by analytic methods. Wolberg would hypnotize them and find a solution. I talked with Dr. Wolberg after his lecture and learned that Dr. Herbert Spiegel conducted courses in hypnosis at Columbia University's College of Physicians and Surgeons. Dr. Spiegel had taught psychoanalysis at the William Alanson White Institute of Psychiatry in New York and now was devoting himself to this method. I had to look at it more closely. I enrolled in Dr. Spiegel's courses.

Undoubtedly you harbor doubts and questions about the efficacy of hypnosis, just as I did and as my patients in analysis at first do. Let me try to dispel the doubts and clear up the misconceptions by dealing, one by one, with the fears and questions I most frequently hear expressed.

1. *"What if I don't wake up from hypnosis?"*

This fear, as pervasive as it is spurious, undoubtedly owes much of its currency to B-movie exploitation.

I recall an incident involving a patient in my office. I had hypnotized him, or rather helped him to hypnotize himself, and informed him that at a given signal from me he would emerge from the state. I gave the signal, and he remained there with his eyes closed, perfectly still. I repeated the instruction, and he continued to remain there in that state.

So then I said to him, "All right, you're going to remain in your present state as long as you like. In your own time you will open your eyelids and feel your old sensations and controls returning."

In about thirty seconds this happened. He said to me, "You know, I was asleep. I remember everything that occurred, your posthypnotic suggestion to me, and then about the point where you began to talk about emerging—poof!—I was out." He had slid from the hypnotic state into sleep.

Now, the two states, hypnosis and sleep, sit side by side like fraternal, certainly not identical, twins. It's easy to slide from hypnosis into sleep, and that can be very helpful for people who are plagued with difficulty in sleeping. This man, being quite tired, had come in from a distant state for this session after only four hours' sleep. So he took the occasion to sleep. I wasn't worried for a moment, because everyone always emerges. (Incidentally, I understand that an offer of $100,000 exists for anyone who does not emerge from the state of hypnosis.)

2. *"Just how does the hypnotic state differ from sleep?"*

The most significant earmark that distinguishes hypnosis from sleep is the matter of enhanced concentration. Sleep is a state of decreased concentration. The state of hypnosis is one of increased concentration. Both are characterized by relaxation of various muscle groups and ultimately of the entire body. But following this total relaxation, hypnosis is a raised state—that is, a higher plane of feeling and thinking, where memory and perception and understanding become sharpened. An opportunity is created to home in on the area you want to explore, whereas sleep is a diffused, generalized, unspecific state of mind.

Some confusion in the public mind may stem from the fact that in both sleep and hypnosis the stimuli and sensations of the external world tend to be screened out—all of them in sleep and all those not directly relevant to the focus of concentration in hypnosis. A horn may sound, a door may slam, there may be noises in the next room. In hypnosis they're relegated to the fringes of awareness, whereas in sleep they're completely masked.

Brain-wave experiments have provided scientific proof of

the difference between the two states: whereas EEG patterns are similar for a subject in a normal waking state and in hypnosis, they are markedly different during sleep.

3. *"What if I don't remember what happens during hypnosis?"*

Questionnaires answered by a group of university psychology students, who are presumably more sophisticated in their understanding of the workings of hypnosis than the general public, revealed that a majority believed that they would not remember in their normal state what happened while they were hypnotized. This is another fallacy. You will remember everything. There are only two situations in which amnesia may occur:

A. If you are hypnotized by someone who plants the posthypnotic suggestion, "You will forget," upon emerging from the state you will tend to carry out the instruction.

B. The highly hypnotizable subjects, the so-called fives, may be regressed to infancy during the state, and when they are no longer in hypnosis will not recall that reliving of early years.

But both of these instances require that a second party be involved in the hypnosis, in the first instance to implant the suggestion of amnesia and in the second to regress the subject. You are interested in hypnotizing yourself not to find out what you were like at the age of two, but to implant suggestions that will bring about the changes in yourself you desire.

4. *"Aren't weak-willed, less intelligent people most easily hypnotized?"*

Exactly the opposite. The best subjects tend to be those of average or above average intelligence, possessed of strong motivation and the ability to concentrate.

5. *"Don't I lose my self-control during hypnosis?"*

Another fallacy. As we said, one is in a state of sharpened awareness, as opposed to being in some fuzzy, confused condition. The person is very alert to what he is trying to change in himself and thus is not in any sense "in the hands of" the hypnotist, if there is one. He is alert to what the hypnotherapist will deliver to him that will be of value to him. This is not a loss of control. It's as if you were listening to a lecture and you were enthralled with the delivery of the man on the platform. You would listen to him with greater sharpness. If, however, the man were to say, "I suggest that you give your whole life over to me, and when you emerge I want you to run to the bank and get me all of your money," no matter how entranced you might be, the suggestion would be siphoned off, set to one side. It just would not fit with your wish to be in charge of your own bank account.

Still, you may think of the stage hypnotist who makes people do silly things. But this *is* a stage experience, and the volunteer is in effect saying, when he steps onto the stage, "I am now a performer and I will act as a performer. I will give up my nonperforming censors and let myself be an actor. If they tell me to be a chicken, I'll be a chicken. If they tell me to be a chair, I'll be a chair." He is voluntarily agreeing to provide entertainment; the hypnotist simply suggests the nature of the entertainment. The commitment is made to perform, not when the volunteer becomes hypnotized, but when he takes the stage. Whereas if one enters the therapist's office in order to quit smoking, he will decline an invitation to act like a chicken. What happens on the stage in hypnosis is conditioned by the circumstances. We have a totally different set of circumstances with the person who says, "I want to give up smoking (or alcohol, or overeating, or whatever the problem is). I hate it; it's ruining my life."

6. *"Can antisocial or immoral behavior be induced under hypnosis?"*

The standard answer is: you cannot be made to do anything under hypnosis you would not do otherwise. After an extensive review of the literature and experiments, Ernest Hilgard concluded:

"The possibility of influencing behavior posthypnotically has both benign and sinister implications. Symptom suppression and habit strengthening are possible beneficial results; imposing antisocial attitudes or even suggesting crimes are among the feared potentials. Reviews of the literature and experiments on suggested antisocial behavior are reassuring. Although there is always the possibility that someone might be led to do something violent or destructive if he is inclined to do it without hypnosis, there is little likelihood of producing antisocial behavior through hypnosis that cannot be produced without it."

Of course, this whole question becomes irrelevant for the person practicing self-hypnosis.

7. *"I smoke because I'm tense and nervous. Smoking relaxes me. What happens if I get rid of my cigarettes but not the underlying cause, the tension that results in my smoking? Don't I develop other problems?"*

This is a most common concern, due largely, I suspect, to the nineteenth-century engineering-influenced thinking mentioned earlier: when you push one lever down, another comes up—the Rube Goldberg stuff of times past. The sciences of physiology, biology and neurology have demonstrated that the human mechanism, in contrast to mechanical gadgets, is not a closed system but an open one: you can quiet a heart problem without requiring the patient to break a leg.

If you consider the difference between the hydraulics thinking of yesterday and the open system reflected in our understanding of today, you find that deeper-lying difficulties are not aggravated when a superficial problem is cleared up; they simply remain untouched. If a person hypnotizes himself in order to eat less so that he will drop weight, it will be for that specific purpose, and it will leave untouched any other problems, such as the possibility that he may hate his mother. That can continue to produce other problems. But it wouldn't mean that he would bounce into some other health-damaging situation. It would simply mean that the deeper difficulty would persist, possibly calling for a more exploratory technique such as psychoanalysis to get it under control.

In fact, rather than new difficulties popping up when self-hypnosis dispels old ones, the opposite is more likely to occur: a "ripple effect" comes into play. As a person gains mastery over one troubling aspect of his behavior, sympathetic ripples seem to be set up that carry over into other areas of concern. The former smoker cuts down on his drinking, the person once afraid of flying sleeps better, etc. As he achieves one goal, there tends to be an enlarged control of other aspects of behavior.

8. *"How is hypnosis generally regarded in the academic and medical communities today?"*

Two answers: acceptance is selectively strong, and scorn is selectively strong.

The practice of hypnosis is now endorsed by the American Medical Association and the British Medical Association, among others. It has earned a place in the curricula of medical schools and universities throughout the world and is taught by scientists trained to be skeptical. Consider Ernest Hilgard, devoting his post-teaching life to research in hypnosis. Consider a man of the stature of Martin Orne, an M.D. and a Ph.D. at the University of Pennsylvania, dedicating both his teaching life and his research career to this material. Then there is Gerald Blum, a prominent researcher in the field of psychology, whose later writing is on hypnosis. And Lewis Wolberg, Herbert Spiegel, Erika Fromm, George Estabrooks—and many other dedicated scientists with impeccable credentials.

On the other hand, there are equally distinguished figures in respectable departments of psychiatry and psychology in universities all over the country who dismiss hypnosis. They say there is no such thing, that it's simply a matter of suggestion, motivation, etc. So the battle rages.

What cannot be ignored is the critical fact that *something* happens during the hypnotic experience. No matter what you call it, regardless of what causes it, however you explain it—something does happen. When Dr. Ralph August's patient sings her way through a Caesarean section without need of chemical anesthetic, there's no denying that something out of the ordinary is at work.

For our purposes here, what's important is results. If you can learn a technique that takes just a few seconds or at most a few minutes a day, and that will relieve you of problems physical and emotional, it matters little what it's called.

9. *"Freud investigated, then rejected hypnosis. Considering what's been learned since his time, what do you think he might say about it today?"*

Freud was first and foremost a researcher. He was trying to understand the human mind. He was not trying to cure. He did get some important clues from hypnosis, especially that there was this thing he called the unconscious; then he went on to devise two other methods, dream analysis and free association, that he felt gave him more information about the human mind than hypnosis did.

I think that if he were to arrange a Rip Van Winkle awakening today, perhaps he'd say, "I observe you people working with hypnosis and I think you're doing well. Sometimes you may achieve results faster than through the long method I devised. I did predict, you know, that hypnosis one day would return as a respectable means of treatment."

However, Freud would probably go on to say that as a method of investigation, as a means of exploring the human psyche, he preferred psychoanalysis. So he might conclude, "Keep on with it, because hypnosis helps people. But I'm in a different business. I'm a searcher for information about the structure of the mind."

Significantly, in his later years Freud did acknowledge the debt he owed hypnosis. "The importance of hypnotism for the history of the development of psychoanalysis," he wrote, "must not be too lightly estimated. Both in theoretic as well as in therapeutic aspects psychoanalysis is the administrator of the estate left by hypnotism."

10. *"Is there any danger in practicing self-hypnosis?"*

To my knowledge, there has never been an instance reported of an individual suffering harm from practicing self-hypnosis. *There will either be favorable results or no results.* I should amend that statement with one caveat: when physical pain is the problem or is part of it, consult a physician before practicing hypnosis. Let there first be competent medical diagnosis and treatment for underlying causes of pain. Later, self-hypnosis may safely be engaged in to remove the *hurt* arising from the pain by reducing the hurt to a feeling of pressure. The continuing pressure—from a headache, say—will indicate that the trouble is still there and should be dealt with medically. (We will have more to say on this in the section on alleviating pain.)

11. *"Wouldn't I be better off going to a hypnotherapist rather than trying to hypnotize myself?"*

To answer that I would like to quote Milton Erickson, one of the foremost medical hypnotists in the country today. In *Advanced Techniques of Hypnosis and Therapy,* Dr. Erickson writes:

"Often, techniques of hypnosis center primarily about what the hypnotist does or says to secure trances, with too little attention directed to what the subject is doing and experiencing. Actually, the development of a trance state is an intrapsychic phenomenon, dependent upon internal processes, and the activity of the hypnotist serves only to create a favorable situation. As an analogy, an incubator supplies a favorable environment for the hatching of eggs, but the actual hatching derives from the development of life processes within the egg."

As explained earlier, a person hypnotizes himself; a hypnotist merely acts as a guide to direct him down the path. There is more than one path, however, and some wind longer to their destination than others. This book will mark the shortest, most direct route I know.

If you really want to be hypnotized, you can do it yourself. I'd like to cite a case of self-hypnosis in which the subject had considerably less direction than the reader will have after finishing this book.

Marjorie is secretary to a doctor friend of mine. On his desk he had an unpublished report on hypnosis I had written, and one day Marjorie picked it up, read it and decided to try it on herself. I learned from the doctor some months later that she was achieving results in hypnotizing herself. What was her problem? She explained to him that she was nervous at home, with two difficulties pressing in on her. One problem was her three active youngsters (I'd call that at least three difficulties right there). Her other concern was that she was about to try out for a singing role in an amateur performance in her Jersey shore community.

On reading my article, she decided to attack her nervousness with self-hypnosis. Now, this early report was on hypnosis itself, without specific mention of *self*-hypnosis. I telephoned her to see how she was doing, and she told me she had simply followed the directions in the article: ". . . roll up your eyes, slowly close your lids, breathe in, hold, exhale, let your eyes relax, let your body float right down through the chair, floating deeper, deeper, floating."

Hers was something of a pioneering effort, since as far as I was able to learn from her she had never heard of self-hypnosis before. I asked her, "How did you emerge from this relaxed state?" She replied, "I don't know; I just sort of decided to come out of it and I did." I told her she was doing well and that if she had any questions to call me.

A few days later she telephoned with this question: "I'm just wondering whether I'm really hypnotizing myself. I seem to be feeling much better, but is it hypnosis?" She asked whether I had any tests to help her tell whether she was actually hypnotizing herself. I told her she was welcome to try a fairly common test:

"After you go through your relaxation and you feel you are thoroughly relaxed, concentrate on either your left or your right arm and hand. Keep your eyes closed and tell yourself that in a while you'll develop movement sensations in the middle finger. And then that these movements will spread and will cause your hand to feel light and buoyant. Your elbow will bend and, almost as if there's a magnet pulling on your wrist, you'll let it float upward, all the way up, higher, higher and higher. If it turns out that somewhat involuntarily the hand seems to rise, you'll know you're hypnotized. But if you have to pull it up voluntarily, you're not. Call me when you like."

Two hours later my phone rang. Somewhat astonished, Marjorie told me, "I had this strange experience: my arm just rose right up. I didn't make it do it; all of a sudden my arm was up there. It was so surprising to me!"

"Well," I responded, "you should have no doubts now about your ability to hypnotize yourself. Keep up the good work."

12. *"How can I be sure I'm really hypnotizing myself?"*

One means is by trying the Arm-Levitation experiment just described. But the surest way I know of telling whether you're experiencing hypnosis is the efficacy of the posthypnotic suggestion. If what you tell yourself during the self-hypnotic exercise happens, then you can be sure it's working. A cautionary note, however: don't expect instant success. Chances are it won't come about after one exercise. Give it time. After all, the habit or fear or whatever it is you want to change has been with you a long time. Give yourself time to banish it—and don't become discouraged if this doesn't happen immediately.

Many people—most, I would say—are surprised that the hypnotic experience isn't more dramatic than it is. They're expecting a flash of lightning and clap of thunder. "I couldn't have been hypnotized; I was aware of everything," is a common observation. Don't expect fireworks. The sensation of hypnosis is most often characterized by a pleasant, detached feeling of tranquillity.

The intensity of the experience can fluctuate widely, not only from person to person, but with you yourself from exercise to exercise and from day to day, depending on your mental and emotional set at the time. Just as your esthetic reaction to the same piece of music and your gustatory pleasure in the same dish can wax and wane, so will your response to the self-hypnotic exercise.

As for myself, I know that sometimes I seem to float right down into the easy chair in my office and at other times my level of awareness appears to be altered scarcely at all. Yet I know, from the empirical proof of the realization of posthypnotic suggestions, that I'm reaching my unconscious mind whether I'm in a deep level of involvement or a shallow one. As Dr. Lewis R. Wolberg has stressed:

"The depth of involvement is not always proportionate to the degree of suggestibility. In other words, even if one goes no deeper than the lightest stages of hypnosis and is merely mildly relaxed, one will still be able to benefit from its therapeutic effects. It is possible with practice to go more deeply into a hypnotic state, but that is really not too important in the great majority of cases."

13. *"Is self-hypnosis really any different from other mind-altering practices such as meditation, Zen and Yoga?"*

All such techniques offer the serious follower an intense personal experience, the opportunity to function on a different plane of consciousness. Therapeutic benefits undoubtedly derive from each.

I feel that self-hypnosis, at least the approach to self-hypnosis we're advocating here, has two distinct advantages over other mind-affecting exercises:

A. Self-hypnosis is a time-saver. Most other methods of altering consciousness call for periods of practice of twenty minutes or more. The self-hypnotic exercise requires approximately thirty seconds. That's not very much time when you consider the benefits such investment buys.

B. Self-hypnosis is very specifically goal-oriented. You practice it with a definite purpose in mind; you want to change something in yourself. Although relaxation, serenity, decreased tension and increased energy are common to all these other approaches, such results appear to be beneficent side effects. However, in self-hypnosis, one may deliberately choose such a result via a posthypnotic suggestion.

14. *"If I can hypnotize myself, is there anything wrong with hypnotizing my wife?"*

The major problem here is that in so doing the person takes on a position of power with respect to his wife. That can be counterproductive. Instead, turn this book over to her. Why? Because this book is an invitation to the reader to take charge of his own life, to use a technique which will enable him to pull himself up by his bootstraps. Actually, the reader would be doing just the opposite of this if he hypnotized his wife. In effect, he'd be saying to her, "Since you can't take charge of your own life, I'll do it for you."

15. *"If I need it, where can I get help with my self-hypnosis?"*

It is my intention and my hope that this book will provide

you with everything you need to know to learn and practice self-hypnosis successfully. Some people may feel more comfortable and more confident with personalized instruction. For these individuals, help is not far away. There now is a large and growing number of hypnotherapists throughout the country specializing in the teaching of a single-session method of self-hypnosis. To find the therapist nearest you, contact your county medical or psychological society or write either of the following organizations:

The Society for Clinical and Experimental Hypnosis
129-A Kings Park Drive
Liverpool, New York 13088

The International Society of Hypnosis
111 North Forty-ninth St.
Philadelphia, Pa. 19139

CHAPTER 3

Just What *Is* Hypnosis?

> *The greatest discovery of my generation is that human beings can alter their lives by altering their attitudes of mind. (William James)*

If you are still fuzzy as to exactly what hypnosis is, join the experts. It is far easier to describe what hypnosis *does* than to say adequately what it *is*. Ask a hundred experts to define the state and you'll get one hundred and one explanations laced with ambiguities, contradictions, "on the other hands" and "I don't knows." Like the three blind men who were asked to describe an elephant after each felt a different part—the trunk, a leg, the tail—the authorities know there is such an animal as hypnosis, but they can't agree on how to describe it. Where they reach consensus, happily, is on the effects of hypnosis, on the fact that something happens as a result of the practice.

Throughout this chapter you will read attempts by authorities—researchers, clinicians, writers in the field—to define the state that for so long has so nimbly evaded defining. I quote them to such a degree for two reasons. One is to show the range of thinking on the nature of the phenomenon. If we were to invite all of the individuals responsible for these definitions into a room and inform them that they would not be permitted to leave until they came up with a mutually acceptable meaning, it would be some elderly personages indeed who finally would emerge.

Secondly, I want to demonstrate that in spite of their differences, a thread of common concepts runs through many of the definitions: *altered state of awareness, focused concentration, susceptibility to suggestion, conscious and unconscious functioning.* Not all authorities incorporate all of these concepts in their thinking, but these or similar phrases crop up with significant frequency.

Logic insists that if we humans wish to communicate with one another with any precision at all, the communicating parties must reach some agreement on what words mean. With this in mind, I hereby plunge into already murky waters to join my colleagues in offering a working definition of hypnosis, certainly not the definitive one but one that will serve our purposes in this book. I find it most useful to view hypnosis as *an intense internal experience wherein the individual shifts to a higher level of attention and concentration and thereby achieves a designated goal.*

By whatever definition, the most important thing about hypnosis is not what it *is* but what it *does.* You might think of it as working as a magnifying glass does. Just as the magnifying

---

Actually, the hypnotic state, like the conscious state and the sleeping state, is extremely complex and involves so many physiological, psychological, and interpersonal factors that no one theory has yet been able to account for all the intricate operations that take place within its range. This does not at all hinder our practical employment of this interesting method. In medicine we utilize many remedies and procedures because they work, even though we may not know exactly why and how they work. Every year, research adds more data to our fund of knowledge, providing an empirical foundation for our pragmatic superstructure. (Lewis R. Wolberg)

---

glass gathers the sun's rays and refracts them into a beam of fire-bright intensity, in self-hypnosis an individual, through focused concentration, burns specific *suggestions* into his *unconscious* mind.

If there were a single key to hypnosis, a solitary secret locked somewhere within its mechanism, that one critical element would be the unconscious mind. The unconscious provides the greatest hidden resource a human being possesses, an inexhaustible and indefatigable servant literally at his beck and call. Tapping this power and harnessing it to effect changes in the individual is the aim of both psychoanalysis and hypnosis. Because the unconscious cloaks itself in so many layers of defense, we seldom glimpse it clearly, but, like hypnosis itself, through its manifestations we know it is there. It is from the camouflaged underground control center of the unconscious that our lives are largely directed—for better or for worse.

Most informed people today, I believe, would accept the theory of the unconscious, though they may find it easier to

---

Hypnosis is the term applied to a unique, complex form of unusual but normal behavior which can probably be induced in all normal persons under suitable conditions and also in many persons suffering from various types of abnormality. It is primarily a special psychological state with certain physiological attributes, resembling sleep only superficially and marked by a functioning of the individual at a level of awareness other than the ordinary conscious state. . . . When hypnotized, or in the hypnotic trance, the subject can think, act and behave in relationship to either ideas or reality objects as adequately as, and usually better than, he can in the ordinary state of awareness. In all probability this ability derives from intensity and restriction of attention to the task in hand, and the consequent freedom from the ordinary conscious tendency to orient constantly to distracting, even irrelevant, reality considerations. (Encyclopedia Britannica)

Hypnotism is simply exaggerated suggestibility. (George H. Estabrooks)

demonstrate than to define, like hypnosis. As one who has wrestled with the unconscious minds of patients day in and day out for twenty years, who has witnessed both the marvels and the havoc it can work, I state without reservation that I am as certain of the existence of the unconscious as I am that dawn brings day.

As to just what it *is,* for our purposes here let us accept a definition from Webster's:

"The sum of all thoughts, memories, impulses, desires, feelings, etc. of which the individual is not conscious but which influence his emotions and behavior; that part of one's psyche which comprises repressed material of this nature."

Although recognition of the unconscious dates back at least to Plato, it was Freud who first effectively articulated the notion that buried beneath the level of awareness lies a multitude of unconscious forces, a host of powerful influences responsible for the bulk of human behavior. This arresting insight apparently came to him as he observed posthypnotic suggestions being followed at a clinic in Nancy, France, in 1889. Freud described the experience in his papers:

"I witnessed the moving spectacle of old Liebault working among the women and children of the laboring classes. I was a spectator of Bernheim's astonishing experiments upon his hospital patients, and I received the profoundest impression of the possibility that there could be powerful mental processes that nevertheless remained hidden from the consciousness of men."

Watching the workings of hypnosis: thus the foundation of modern psychoanalytic theory was laid.

As the word itself suggests, you are not aware of what's going on in the unconscious, but something is happening on a level below awareness. The air we breathe might be a useful analogy. We don't see it, but it's there, whirling around at a great clip, producing changes in our bodies. Without awareness—unconsciously—we breathe it, otherwise we would die.

The late psychoanalyst Edmund Bergler wrote: "Psycho-analytic interpretations are powerful—they're not just words, for they make the unconscious conscious, and they will cut down the length and frequency of the difficulty."

The same can be said of self-suggestions administered during the elevated state of self-hypnosis. While they don't "make the unconscious conscious," such suggestions do reach the unconscious and modify conscious behavior, sometimes swiftly, sometimes slowly. Thus, one makes a suggestion to himself, and the next day little seems to be happening. However, there is a power at work. Think of a spaceship. The occupants may have no sensation of movement, but the vehicle is hurtling through space nevertheless.

When delivered during self-hypnosis, suggestions become more effective, more highly charged than suggestions made to oneself without benefit of the raised state that characterizes hypnosis. This is why self-hypnosis has so much more to give than other forms of self-help that do not tap the unconscious, that rely on conscious effort alone to succeed.

In working with the unconscious, I have found that rather than constituting separate or alternate approaches, analysis and hypnosis seem to complement each other in a yin-and-yang unity to help people. In analysis we point out the nega-

---

All of the various mesmeric, hypnotic, and verbal suggestive induction procedures have only one objective: to help promote this state of single-mindedness, of exclusively concentrated attention, letting other ideas pass into torpid oblivion. Because the monoideized attention has heightened the intensity of the one focal or dominant idea, the power of the imagination on mind and body is considerably greater than in the ordinary waking state, and thus suggestions are likely to initiate correspondingly greater influence. (Ronald E. Shor)

---

*Hypnosis is largely a question of your willingness to be recep-
tive and responsive to ideas, and to allow these ideas to act upon
you without interference. These ideas we call suggestions.
(Andre M. Weitzenhoffer and Ernest R. Hilgard)*

tive; once the unconscious causes of an unwanted symptom
are made conscious, the symptom is more easily dispatched.
Hypnosis ignores the negative and, in the words of a popular
song of the 1940s, accentuates the positive by implanting
affirmative suggestions in the brain, instructing it to respond
as it has been programmed to do. Put another way, analysis
goes in from below and *extracts;* hypnosis comes in at the top
and *implants.*

Let us turn to the machinery of the self-hypnotic exercise. We will now describe the method as I employ it and
teach it to patients in my office, and then in later chapters we
will expand on its mechanics and explain in more detail how
you can most effectively apply the exercise to meet your own
wants and needs.

We might divide the hypnotherapy into five parts: *induction*
of the hypnotic state, use of the *syllogism, self-image,* implanting
posthypnotic suggestions, and *emergence* from the state.

Let us deal with the stages one by one.

1. *Induction.* Some therapists use the word "trance," but I
find the word misleading, connoting as it does a stupor or
coma, a loss of awareness, which as we have seen is the exact
opposite of what actually occurs during the experience. I

*Hypnosis is not sleep. Whatever sleep is, hypnosis is not. In an
operational sense, hypnosis is a response to a signal from
another or to an inner signal, which activates a capacity for a
shift of awareness in the subject and permits a more intensive
concentration upon a designated goal direction. . . . To put it
succinctly, hypnosis is an altered state of attention which approaches peak concentration capacity. (Herbert Spiegel)*

. . . a state of intensified attention and receptiveness, and an increased responsiveness to an idea or to a set of ideas. (Milton H. Erickson)

prefer such terms as "hypnotic state," "relaxed state" or "raised state" to describe the condition.

There are many induction methods, several of them through sight, *e.g.*, staring at some object such as a whirling disk, a metronome or a drawing of an apparently winking eye, etc. Or the subject may gaze at a pocket watch swinging back and forth on a chain. The monotony, as he concentrates on it, sends him into the hypnotic state.

There are methods other than visual. In the "stiff-arm" method, the person is told he will not be able to bend his outstretched arm. Also, there's the "linking of hands," where he's told he cannot pull his intertwined fingers apart.

There is nothing sacred in the selection of the induction method. If it works, it's the right method. The main criterion should be that the subject finds it comfortable. If a person wants to be hypnotized and is ready to be hypnotized, he will be hypnotized, regardless of the induction technique employed. All too much attention has been lavished on external aids such as spinning wheels and dangling watches, when the sole determinant of whether the subject will be hypnotized lies within the subject himself. He himself does the hypnotizing, not the gadgets or the second person, the so-called hypnotist.

The induction method I have found most effective and the one my patients find easiest to use themselves is the Eye-Roll.[1] It will be discussed fully in Chapter 5, "The Method." Briefly, it goes like this:

The subject looks up toward his eyebrows, toward the top of his head, as high as he can. Holding his eyes in that position, he slowly closes his lids, takes a deep breath and holds it. He exhales and lets his eyes relax and lets his body "float." At the

---

[1] Herbert Spiegel, M.D., *Manual for Hypnotic Induction Profile* (New York: Soni Medica, Inc., 1970).

same time, he imagines that he's on a beach or in some situation where he feels most comfortable and at peace.

2. *Syllogism*. After assuming the hypnotic state, the subject is ready for any hypnotherapy he may wish to use. It is administered first in the form of a syllogism, that Gibraltar of deductive logic. You may recall a classic example of a syllogism:

> *Socrates was a man.*
> *All men are mortal.*
> *Therefore, Socrates was mortal.*

If the subject is practicing self-hypnosis for something like weight reduction, then the syllogism will go this way:

"For my body, not for me but for my body, the intake of certain foods and the eating of food in great amounts are poisons.

"I need my body to live.

"Insofar as I want to live, I will protect my body."

3. *Self-image*. A second part of the hypnotherapeutic approach I favor is projecting a self-image onto an imaginary screen. As the patient or subject sits there in this pleasant state and with his eyes closed, he is asked to consider that there is a movie screen on the wall in from of him and that he can project an image of himself onto the screen.

... temporary condition of altered attention in the subject which may be induced by another person and in which a variety of phenomena may appear spontaneously or in response to verbal or other stimuli. These phenomena include alterations in consciousness and memory, increased suggestibility to suggestion, and the production in the subject of responses and ideas unfamiliar to him in his usual state of mind. Further, phenomena such as anesthesia, paralysis, muscle rigidity and vasomotor changes can be produced and removed in the hypnotic state. (American Medical Association)

Can he see himself there? When he can, he's told to fill out that figure, let it really become three-dimensional, tall, powerful. Take a black crayon and outline the figure so that it stands out from the screen. Now it becomes his privilege to pick up the microphone, so to speak, and tell that figure how he wants it to live. This is his opportunity to program into his computer anything he wishes for himself.

I'd like to explain just why I like this imagery technique so much. A patient of mine said that his car had broken down a couple of days previously, causing him no little inconvenience and aggravation. When he started out from his home on Long Island that morning, he began to fear that it would happen again. As he grew more and more tense and "sort of shivery," he stopped to engage in such an exercise that we're now discussing, and he threw on the "screen" a picture of himself "as a hero—powerful, strong, calm. Nothing can move me." He found that he was able to proceed into the city with ease.

This kind of thing follows an ancient dictum—*picture it and it shall be; picture it and it will happen*—that I find very useful. If we take the trouble to watch our thoughts, we find that we undeliberately and automatically do a lot of such picturing, but of a negative sort. A person will say, "I must have had a premonition: I visualized that I was in an automobile accident, and then I was."

What's happening? The person was unconsciously and inadvertently letting a negative picture develop in his mind, such that he may indeed steer his car in the direction that will bring on an accident.

The essence (of hypnosis) lies in the experimental fact of a quantitative shift in the upward direction which may result from the hypnotic procedure. So far as the writer can see, this quantitative phenomenon alone remains of the once imposing aggregate known by the name of hypnosis. But this undoubted fact is quite sufficient to give significance and value to the term. (Clark L. Hull)

. . . nothing but an aspect of conditioning. (Andrew Salter)

If this is true, and I am convinced that it is, why not reverse the procedure and deliberately develop great *positive* pictures and bring those about? There's nothing magical about it; if a person wants to be thin, for instance, he simply pictures himself as thin. The expression goes, "Think thin." And that has been shown again and again to be a very useful rearrangement of the molecules of one's head—and body.

Positive mental pictures thus provide another mode of increasing the input into the computer of the unconscious. All computers are, at best, poor copies of the brain, so why should I not put as much positive information into this computer, my head, as into a machine? If I put it there in the form of a thought, that's a good start. If I add words to it, that's helpful. If I take the additional step of providing an image, a photograph—better still, a *moving picture*—then I'm increasing many times the likelihood of getting the results I seek.

4. *Posthypnotic Suggestions.* After the syllogism and the self-imagery come suggestions designed to be carried out after emerging from the exercise. Let the self-hypnotist tell himself that overeating, for instance, is something he will no longer find consonant with his way of life. He will find that it is easier and easier to limit the amounts and kinds of foods he eats; that turning away from the table will become simple for him; that he will find himself gaining greater and greater control over himself and his life; that if there are setbacks, as there are

. . . an altered state of the organism originally and usually produced by a repetition of stimuli in which suggestion (no matter how defined) is more effective than usual. Such a definition as this is admittedly ringed with if's and but's and questions of how, what, and why, and is more descriptive than explanatory. (F. L. Marcuse)

There is nothing mysterious about hypnosis. Its application is based solely on the known psychological relationship between the conscious and the subconscious minds. The subconscious, having no power to reason, accepts and acts upon any fact or suggestion given to it by the conscious mind. (Frank S. Caprio and Joseph R. Berger)

bound to be, he will learn from them, etc. These are obviously positive suggestions that are in keeping with his aim in practicing self-hypnosis.

Does it all sound too simple to be effective? If so, don't forget two critical points: that the cumulative power grows from the repetition of suggestions and, most important, that the simple-sounding suggestions are administered during the raised state of hypnosis, when the unconscious mind is most susceptible to positive implants.

So suggestions are a third therapy method, along with the syllogism and self-imagery, administered within the induced state.

5. *Emergence.* The final step is emergence from the hypnotic state. It is accomplished simply by reversing the procedure of induction by counting backward from three: "Three, get ready; two, keeping your lids closed, slowly raise your eyes; and one, slowly open your lids. Take a deep breath, make fists with your hands, raise arms overhead and yawn. Lower your arms and open your hands." The subject now finds he has regained his usual sensations and control.

I'd like to return for a moment to criteria for the raised state, since so much confusion exists concerning the peculiar

Hypnosis is a consent state of physiological relaxation where the subject allows the critical censor of the mind to be by-passed to a greater, or lesser, degree. . . . We could even go so far as to say that hypnosis is "preventive psychological medicine." (Peter Blythe)

state we call hypnosis. How will you know for certain you're hypnotizing yourself?

One criterion is highly subjective: how you feel during and immediately after performing the exercise. We mentioned earlier that a certifiably hypnotized subject often refuses to believe he was hypnotized. Others emerge from the state with an exultant "Wow!" For the most part, individuals describing their sensations use words such as "peace," "comfortable," "distance from problems," "relaxed," "floating."

From my own experience (I hypnotize myself every night, to increase effectiveness in patient healing and also to invite sleep), I observe that I feel a sense of removal when in this state. Problems just seem to be down there someplace, as one reduces automobiles to toy-car size when gazing down into the street from a tall building.

But there are varying degrees of this state. It's relative rather than absolute, and you won't have the same feelings with each experience. Often it's quite undramatic, but on other occasions, when you shift psychic gears smoothly and ascend to an elevated plane, you will achieve a feeling of synchrony with self.

Sometimes there is an exultant feeling in the aftermath of certain self-hypnotic experiences—not all the time, but on some occasions—a sense that a new synthesis has taken place. I don't want to get too rhapsodic, but such a feeling following the heightened state can convince a person he has indeed experienced an altered state of consciousness. But remember, such a feeling isn't essential to being hypnotized. A feeling of increased relaxation can be an equally valid indication.

A complete theory of hypnosis would doubtless have much to say about the relationship of the hypnotic state to known processes going on within the brain and nervous system, the various parameters influencing hypnotic performances, the subordinate processes of induction and trance deepening; however, such a complete theory is not available. (Josephine R. Hilgard)

It is recognized that there is no generally accepted definition of hypnosis, though considerable consensus exists at a descriptive level. (Martin T. Orne)

The main proof of the hypnotic state is the carrying out of the self-administered posthypnotic suggestion. Let me give an example. I was treating a woman who had a drinking problem. I instructed her that before her self-hypnosis she should go to her refrigerator and line up two bottles, one of the beer of her preference, the second a bottle of milk or a favorite juice. Her self-administered therapy, a posthypnotic suggestion administered during the state of relaxation, went like this: "When I emerge from this state, at any time from now to bedtime when I have an urge for a glass of beer, on opening the refrigerator door I will find myself impelled invariably to the milk [or the juice]."

This turned out to be the case. She found that the hand almost had a mind of its own. She'd go for the milk and pour it into a glass. A backup suggestion to this, as she was reaching into the refrigerator, was the thought crossing her mind: "Protect my body." Any reader who found himself in the position where, as he reaches for one bottle the hand swings over to the other, would have graphic proof that he's following a suggestion he made to himself while in the hypnotic state.

Another manifestation of the hypnotic state is the relief of symptoms. I'm thinking of a friend who had dived into a

It is a somewhat altered state of consciousness and altered awareness, although the conscious mind is still present. We might compare it to a teeter-totter. In the waking state the conscious mind is at the high end of the teeter-totter and the subconscious mind at the low end. Under hypnosis they reverse and the subconscious is at the high end and the conscious part at the low end, but it is still present. Thoughts rise from the inner mind into consciousness. (Leslie M. LeCron)

*. . . an altered state within which suggestions have a peculiarly
potent effect. (K. S. Bowers)*

swimming pool, hit his head and scrambled his vertebrae. An
operation was performed on his neck, after which I visited
him in the hospital twice. The first hypnotherapy was for
depression over his physical state; the second was for pain.

During that second visit, I instructed him in self-hypnosis
with the following posthypnotic therapy: "When I emerge
from this state I will feel a coolness through my neck, a
heaviness through my neck. It will feel comfortable, rested,
cool and heavy." On emerging from the raised state he did
indeed feel heaviness without pain.

The same technique is applicable to anxiety, nervousness,
tension, fears or phobias of any sort. If they are relieved, you
know the method is working.

In short, the actual process of self-hypnosis, though usually
a quiet, undramatic experience, is one characterized by two
distinct features:

  1. There is a different feeling in the experience itself, and
  2. The results can be striking.

Hypnosis is a subjective experience, different for each one
of us, just as each one of us has a face and fingerprints that are
distinctively his. The prime objective measurement we will
seek is a very concrete one: accomplishment. If you get results,
hypnosis works—however it is defined.

CHAPTER 4

What Hypnosis Can Do for You

In my files, tucked away for possible reference but also for a smile whenever I dig them out, I keep a packet of newspaper clippings concerning the accomplishments of hypnosis. These articles run the gamut from the sublime ("Self-Hypnosis Can Help You Spend Less $") to the ridiculous ("Hypnosis Is Said to Help People Win in Las Vegas"), with all stops in between ("Hypnosis Can Get Rid of Warts, Say Scientists").

Scarcely a week passes that doesn't bring to light new, often exotic, applications of the hypnotic technique, *e.g.,* for breast enlargement. Leslie M. LeCron, a clinical psychologist and teacher of hypnosis in California, writes:

"Breast development by hypnotic suggestion has been reported in many instances, and of seven cases among my own patients, six found an increase in measurement from one and a half inches to more than two inches. To say that these girls were pleased is putting it mildly."

I'm neither advocating nor endorsing the employment of self-hypnosis for inflation of bustline or bank account; the point is that the boundaries of its application are flexible, to be set solely by the imagination of the practitioner.

Potential uses, of course, must fall within the confines of the credible. One middle-aged man, a bus driver, came to me with the expectation that he could learn hypnosis to "turn my head around" in order to become a successful writer overnight, without practice or education. Hypnosis can't do that (though after reading some best sellers you may conclude that hypnosis—in fact, anything—would have helped).

But it can do a lot. In *Hypnosis—Fact and Fiction,* F. L. Marcuse wrote, "Even if one were to reduce the number of claims concerning the efficacy of hypnosis by 75 percent and the degree of success in individual cases by a similar amount, the results would still be impressive and would indicate the therapeutic value of hypnosis."

Indeed they would. I find the mode so beneficial that I try to get every patient I see to learn self-hypnosis. It's like reading, writing and arithmetic: an extra arrow in one's quiver, the uses of which increase greatly in years to come.

My own patients practice the technique for a whole spectrum of problems, most frequently on habits such as smoking, drinking and overeating. And there is the area of emotional disturbance: phobias, excessive anger, tension, depression. We have physical complaints, including pain, allergies, insomnia and fatigue, along with such sexual disruptions as impotence, homosexuality, frigidity and premature ejaculation. One patient may wish to tone down his aggression, another to treat his timidity.

I would suggest that you focus on one specific aspect of your life over which you would like to gain more mastery. There may be several problem areas you wish to confront, but they should be dealt with consecutively, not simultaneously. The reason is twofold.

First, to the degree we understand it, the unconscious is not equipped to handle complex problems, just to act on simple, direct suggestions. Remember, it is the primitive part of you; it has more in common with the first grader than with the graduate student.

I had a patient who was performing self-hypnosis on two counts: for a drinking problem and for tension. He reported niggling results, so I questioned him on just how he went about his self-treatment. It turned out he was mixing the two, that is, he would say during the exercise, "For my body, both tension and alcohol are poisons." By lumping the two complaints together, he was asking too much of the unconscious. When he split them up into two distinct moments of concentration, he achieved his desired aims.

On the other hand, there is no law against putting two problems back to back *as long as each is kept separate.* Suppose a person wants to solve two problems within the same time span—for example, fear of flying and smoking. He may begin, "For my 'outer covering,' not for myself but for this object in which I live, smoking is a poison." Then he completes that syllogism: "I need my body, my 'outer covering,' to live. To the degree that I want to live, I will protect my body as I would protect [name of a loved one]." While still feeling quite relaxed, he may then say, "I'm flying tomorrow. For my psychic health, this view of the airplane as an enemy is a kind of poison." Then he completes that syllogism: "I need my psychic health to live contentedly. To the degree I want to live contentedly, I will protect my psychic health."

He's presenting two different subject matters to his unconscious at separate times—just moments apart, but nevertheless separate and distinct. Since the unconscious is unacquainted with time, as long as the two subjects are dealt with individually and in full, there is no confusion: no fusion, so no confusion.

The second reason for taking one problem at a time is that, as you overcome one difficulty, there tends to be an overlap of success into other areas and additional problems seem to fade away, unattended and unmourned. As one conquers a negative habit—smoking, drinking or overeating, for example— the feeling of strength that emerges tends to ripple over to other areas of living. Where results are experienced, one says, "Hey, I see that I can control my destiny after all. I'm not at the mercy of either internal or external stimuli. I have a choice." This pulling together of the loose strings of one's existence often happens slightly below the level of consciousness.

Example: the case of the homosexual I treated who was troubled by his obsessive, agonizing fantasy of flagellation. After first learning then successfully practicing self-hypnosis to rid himself of this fantasy, he remarked one day:

"I'm amazed at the ease with which I've handled other difficulties that used to cause me so much trouble. For example, setting out this morning at 6:30, walking along in the cold, I found my eye was itching. Where previously I would have made a big fuss about this—I'd swear, rub it and otherwise make myself miserable—I just let it stay and it was gone in a minute."

That somewhat homely example represents a "ripple" from the ego-strength gained by overcoming his "presenting" symptom. The "eye-itch cure" that this man allowed himself seems such a minor thing, but to him it was important because it proved that the benefits of his self-hypnosis carried over into unplanned areas.

Just what is it in yourself that you would like to change? Most complaints, I find, fall into four general categories of concern: Habits, Emotions, Physical Disorders and Sexual Problems. Each basic grouping would include a number of specific difficulties:

HABITS
1. Smoking
2. Drinking (alcoholic or nonalcoholic)
3. Overeating
4. Drugs
5. Procrastination
6. Stuttering, Nail Biting, and Other Nervous Habits

EMOTIONS
1. Fears and Phobias
2. Sadness or Depression
3. Anger (Hostility), Irritability, Hate
4. Shyness (Timidity)
5. Nervousness, Anxiety, Tension

PHYSICAL
1. Pain
2. Allergies and Colds
3. Insomnia
4. Tiredness (Fatigue)
5. Hiccups
6. Itching
7. Asthma

SEXUAL
1. Low Sexual Urge
2. Impotence
3. Difficulty in Ejaculating
4. Orgasmic Difficulty in Women
5. Premature Ejaculation
6. Homosexuality

Hypnosis can be effective with all of these if the problem is not wound so tightly in the coils of repression that some form of "depth therapy" must be used to unsnarl it. Sex, for instance, is so entwined with deep feelings originating very early in life that sexual problems offer the greatest challenge. Sometimes—not always but sometimes—hypnosis in conjunction with analysis is called for to handle sexual difficulties.

I'm thinking of a man who came to me for psychoanalytic treatment of a potency problem. The critical material that proved instrumental in enabling him to become potent once again had been brought out in analysis, but was hidden in a thicket of general material concerning his early life. We then invoked hypnosis to pinpoint the pertinent issue. The beauty of hypnosis is that the person in that raised state seems to go directly to a "keynotive" memory presented in the analytic session, one that will enable inner energy to be released so that the person may engage in productive activity.

In addition to his potency problem, this man desired to master both smoking and fear of flying. His work required that he travel a great deal, and he found that trains were consuming too much of his time. Using hypnosis on each of these problems successively—taking them not together, but first one and then the other—he found that he could rather easily clear them up. His impotence took a little longer than the other two, but he soon was able to conquer that as well.

This may be a good place to dispose of the credo, common among analysts, that conscious insight must necessarily precede symptom removal. Desirable as insight obviously is for the functioning of a well-rounded, healthy personality, troubling symptoms can be eliminated without the individual gaining insight into why he harbors them. You can stop smoking without understanding why you smoke, refrain from overeat-

ing without uncovering your reasons for eating too much,
sleep soundly without knowing why you toss and turn, etc. Get
rid of the symptom, and *then* dig for root causes if you wish.

True, a self-damaging symptom can be just one piece of a
puzzle of rather extensive personality disorder, one of many
attendant problems that may require psychoanalysis. One
man came to me with a drinking problem—that's all he wanted
from me consciously. But after one interview it became appar-
ent that there was much more that needed doing. He was a
lawyer, and his troubles with his fellow lawyers weren't solved
by eliminating his drinking problem. Nor were his problems
with his wife. Unless he did something about those, he would
use them later as excuses to begin drinking again. In addition
to dropping his addiction to alcohol, he needed more work to
uproot attendant problems.

Then there is the case of the woman who had gone to a
therapist and been hypnotized out of smoking. A year later
she was abandoned by the man she had been living with. Upset
by this rejection, she began to smoke again. She returned to
the therapist and reached a decision to smoke until the feelings about her man were resolved. In this case, the judgment
was made that the symptom was needed in order to replace
her lost love. (Some clinicians might make something of the
cigarette as a phallic symbol, but in any case there was a vacuum in her life that the cigarette now filled.)

In a case like this, hypnosis will simply be powerless to
remove a symptom clung to for a deep reason. Such a "deep
reason" must be uncovered and taken out from below through
depth therapy before hypnotherapy can put anything in at the
top. I had a patient who pulled out all of the hair on her head
because of a disturbed relationship with her mother. Another
patient, a man, talked incessantly ("logorrhea") because of
problems he had with his father. Both cases called for depth
therapy before hypnotherapy. In the vast majority of cases,
however, no such question of a deep-rooted psychic need
emerges.

So, generally speaking, it's not the type of problem—be it
habit, emotional disorder or bodily complaint—that deter-
mines the efficacy of hypnosis, but rather the depth of the

problem and the hypnotizability of the subject. A person of low hypnotizability will require more inductions of self-hypnosis than a highly susceptible subject in order to firm up any change, whether physical or emotional.

Although we devote considerable attention in this book to gaining mastery over the specific physical and emotional problems listed above—eliminating the negative—we will also work on building up talents and attributes you might already possess but would like to strengthen—accentuating the positive. These are classified generally as feelings and attitudes, and skills. These two basic categories are further divided into the following subjects:

POSITIVE FEELINGS AND ATTITUDES
1. Love and Warmth
2. Good Humor
3. Tact
4. Poise and Courage
5. Ambition

SKILLS OF MIND AND BODY
1. Athletic
2. Mechanical
3. Mental
4. Efficiency and Organizational Ability
5. Work Performance
6. Creative
7. Time Distortion

You may be the type of person who wishes he could feel a little more warmth toward other people, be somewhat more accepting of them rather than on his guard against them. Or you may want to feel more cheerful as you move through the sometimes monotonous routine of your daily life. Perhaps your ambition could use a boost. Self-hypnosis can help with them all.

In the business world, it can be employed on every rung of the corporate ladder, from secretary to chairman of the board. For the former, the technique can be helpful as an aid in learning and polishing such skills as shorthand and typing. For the executive, anxiety over a coming meeting, for example, may be a problem. I have a patient who has a tendency to tighten up and not deliver his best on such occasions. Self-hypnosis helps him to glide through these turbulent waters unscathed, or at least less scathed.

It can also help you improve your performance in sports and other recreational activities by diminishing such impediments as anxiety, tension and lack of confidence, and, through focused concentration and positive image implants, it can help you approach your full potential. These elements are similarly employed effectively in learning to play a musical instrument, as well as improving memory and concentration.

Another interesting benefit is the matter of time distortion. In practicing it, the individual instructs his unconscious during the self-hypnotic exercise that a few minutes of practice on a musical instrument, for example, will bring the same progress that usually comes after an hour of practicing or, as applied to study, an hour's review of material to be covered in an exam will equal a night of cramming. Time distortion can be used in reverse as well, to telescope the time spent in the dentist's chair, perhaps. A report even suggests that Russia has taught cosmonauts to incorporate time distortion in their self-hypnosis in order to make the time in a space capsule seem shorter.

To reiterate: we need not know exactly how the mind functions in order to benefit from its working. There is simply no escaping the empirical fact that the way we think affects the way we feel and the way we behave. The person with a bright, optimistic and enthusiastic approach to life is one who is likely to enjoy success in life. Conversely, the person who starts the day in the dumps, pessimistic about what he may accomplish and fearful of what may befall him, is not likely to be surprised.

If a positive approach is not part of your mental makeup now, and if you're happy being miserable—"very glad to be unhappy," as the song goes—stop reading now. But if you truly *want* to work changes in yourself and if you believe you can change for the better, you are ready now to learn, step by step, a simple but potent method of self-hypnosis for self-mastery.

CHAPTER 5

The Method

There is nothing sacred about any one method of inducing hypnosis—getting to your destination is the important thing, not the route you take to get there. No induction technique will guarantee greater success than another. However, some methods work faster and are easier to practice than others and therefore, to my mind, are more practical. The technique I favor and the one I am teaching in this book is both swift and simple.

The first thing you should do in preparation for practicing the self-hypnotic exercise is to pinpoint one goal you wish to achieve, be it a habit you want to break or some other aspect of your being, physical or attitudinal, that you wish to alter. You can derive benefit from the exercise even without such a specific purpose in mind, but since the method to be learned here is tailor-made for goal achievement and since most people presumably can dig down within themselves to find *something* they're not entirely happy with, we will assume that you want to employ self-hypnosis to effect some definite change in yourself.

For illustrative purposes in learning the technique of self-hypnosis, let us say you want to stop smoking. You know it's harmful to your health. You know it's offensive to others. You *may* know that its psychological roots reach back to infancy and a desire for oral gratification. You've tried to quit or to cut down, but with little or no success. By trying self-hypnosis, the only thing you have to lose is a bad habit. In its place, you can expect not only to gain better health but at the same time to build self-respect, which will ripple out and benefit you in other ways.

In later chapters we will explain exactly how to adapt the exercise to goals other than smoking, but for now, if the termination of smoking is not your goal, simply substitute your own problem, *e.g.,* "overeating," "overdrinking," "fear of flying," "insomnia," etc., whenever you see "smoking" in our instructions.

Just as you would learn any new skill or game, you should begin by learning the fundamentals of self-hypnosis thoroughly. As you become comfortable with the technique and more adept at practicing it, you will be able, even encouraged, to take shortcuts. Having first mastered the rules, you may then mold the exercise to conform to your own needs and personality. But first learn the alphabet before writing the book.

In time you should be able to engage in the exercise nearly anywhere: at the office, in a restaurant, on the train or plane. But to learn it most easily and to help you gain confidence in its use, you should start by finding yourself a relatively quiet and secluded spot for practice. An easy chair, particularly one with a footrest or one that partially reclines, is ideal. Whatever and wherever, the site should be one where you can make yourself thoroughly comfortable and where you can be alone and free from interruption. In the early stages, until you absorb the technique and feel completely at ease with it, you should allow yourself several minutes for each session. After a few learning sessions, each experience should take no more than a minute, and even this brief period will soon shrink to thirty seconds.

The main reason the early sessions will require more time is that you must learn to relax, for relaxation is important as a prelude to the hypnotic state. You may think you already know how to relax, but unless you're one of a very slim minority, you really don't. People speak of "relaxing" on the golf course or over a game of bridge or even at a movie. Such pursuits are worthwhile and even necessary diversions from the pressures and routine of our often stressful workaday lives. But this is not relaxing in the sense we mean in hypnosis. As we employ it here, "relaxation" means the absence of strain or tension—and such a state is more easily articulated than accomplished.

Entire books have been written on the subject of relaxation, including Edmund Jacobson's authoritative *You Must Relax.* (That's not *You* Should *Relax* or *Try to Relax,* but *You* Must *Relax.*) More recently, Herbert Benson's popular *The Relaxation Response* has also proved most helpful. It is Dr. Jacobson's method of progressively relaxing separate muscle groups, starting with the feet and climbing upward through the limbs and trunk to the head, that I teach my patients to use in their self-hypnosis.

You must relax for two reasons. Relaxation, reaching its apogee in sleep, is an end in itself, a restorative balm to both mind and body. Furthermore, as employed in hypnosis, relaxation clears a pathway to the unconscious mind, where suggestions can more readily be accepted and acted upon.

As explained by Herman S. Schwartz in his useful guide, *The Art of Relaxation,* "The best results from constant auto-suggestion are obtained while we are in a state of thorough relaxation, when the mental 'censor' is off guard. Then our thoughts can find their way without hindrance into the sub-conscious mind."

Now, to relax.

Begin by making yourself as comfortable as you can. We will assume that there is a footrest of some kind for your feet to lie on. They should rest side by side and uncrossed, a few inches apart. Your arms should also lie in repose, your left arm on the left armrest of the chair, your right arm on the right armrest. Next, lean your head back and let it recline against the head-rest or the back of the chair.

You are not yet relaxed. It is harder than you might suspect, unless you faint, to get your entire body relaxed. Eschewing fainting, we concentrate on relaxing one part of the body at a time. Start with your left leg and foot. Lift your foot a couple of inches off the footrest, hold it in the air for a few seconds, then let the leg fall heavily of its own weight back to the footrest. Rest. Then, the right leg. Lift the right foot three or four inches in the air, hold it there for several seconds, then let it drop back to the chair. Kerplunk.

Now, without taking the left foot off the footrest, just *imagine* that you're lifting it into the air. There's a slight tension in the leg, a slight tension in the foot. Relax. Leaving your right foot on the footrest, envision lifting the leg into the air. Again, a slight tension. Relax.

Next, go to the left arm. Lift your arm several inches in the air, hold it there for a few seconds, then let it fall back to the armrest, lifeless. Do the same with your right arm: up a few inches off the armrest, hold, and drop back onto the armrest.

Leave the left arm in place there on the armrest, but imagine that you're about to lift the arm. There's a slight tension in the arm. Now release. Repeat the mental image of lifting your right arm a few inches in the air while leaving it in place on the chair arm. Release that tension and relax.

Turn your attention now to your waistline. Pull your stomach and lower back out from the chair, hold, and drop back. Then, remaining in place, just feel a slight tension through your midsection as if you were about to rise. Release. Next, move your shoulders and chest away from the chair, hold a moment and fall back. Without moving, leave your shoulders and chest in place and imagine pulling away from the chair, creating a slight tension. Hold. Relax.

Finally, the head. Take it off the headrest or back of the chair, bring it forward a few inches and let it flop back. Then just imagine doing so. There's a slight tension. Relax. Without moving your head, tighten all of your facial muscles, pulling your features taut, taut, then let them relax. A slight tension in the face now, around the eyes, through the nose and mouth. Release.

Your entire body now is relaxed and heavy. From the top of your head and your face and neck, through your shoulders and chest and arms and midsection, down into your legs and feet, your whole body is heavy and warm, sinking right down into the chair. Take a moment to enjoy this heavy, warm, relaxed sensation. Your body seems to be floating down, down, down, right down into the chair.

Now for the induction process itself. It has three stages, to be executed to a count of three:

ONE. Roll your eyes up toward your eyebrows, as high as you can get them. Try to see the top of your head.

TWO. With your eyes still gazing upward, slowly close your eyelids and, at the same time, take a deep breath.

THREE. Exhale. Let your eyes relax. Let your body float.

So, as you see, at the count of ONE, you do one thing: roll your eyes upward. At the count of TWO, you do two things: close your eyes and take a deep breath. And at the count of THREE, you do three things: exhale, relax your eyes and let your body float.

It's a very pleasant feeling, to be so relaxed and to feel your body seem to float right down into that easy chair. Now, while in this comfortable state, indulge yourself and take a little imaginary vacation. In your mind's eye, picture yourself in a place where you have been or would like to go, some spot where you can be perfectly at ease and at peace with yourself and the world.

Many people see themselves lying on a quiet beach, the sun warm, cooling breezes wafting in, waves gently lapping. Others envision a secluded retreat in the woods. Someone else imagines himself luxuriating in a large, warm pool. Choose your own vacation spot and see yourself there. It's free.

Now, as you picture yourself at the pleasant site of your own choosing, your body continues to float down, down into the chair. Your body is almost a thing apart from you now. You can leave it in place and remove yourself slightly from it. You can now give your body instructions as to how you want it to live. I suggest you give it instructions in three steps, in the form of a syllogism:

FIRST STEP. "For my body, not for me but for my body, smoking is a poison."

SECOND STEP. "I need my body to live."

THIRD STEP. "To the degree I want to live, I will protect my body as I would protect ———."

And here you say to yourself the name of someone very dear to you. It may be a child, a parent, any loved one—even a pet. To carry the greatest emotional power it should be someone close to you, one whose welfare concerns you deeply.

Some readers, however, may not feel very strongly about anyone, or else they may have ambivalent feelings toward the person closest to them. If you have such doubts, it's best to omit ". . . as I would protect ————" and simply end the syllogism with ". . . protect my body."

After the syllogism, I have a recommendation that will enhance the experience of self-hypnosis, while at the same time strengthening the verbal implants you administer to yourself during the exercise. It's an adaptation of a practice I feel safe in saying all of us engage in numberless times every day, but usually not with a purpose in mind: fantasizing.

I'm suggesting that you harness your fantasies and put them to work for you. To explain: when our untethered minds are allowed to wander, they tend to conjure up scenes rather than words. When you think about what you plan to do this weekend, you don't simply say to yourself, "I'm going out to a good dinner, then I'm going to that movie I've been wanting to see."

Instead, you're more likely to picture yourself, in your mind's eye, at a favorite restaurant. The company is pleasant, the atmosphere relaxed. The waiter brings your favorite food and places it in front of you. You can almost smell the aroma and savor the taste. Then you see yourself in the darkened theater. The seat is plush and comfortable, and you're thoroughly enjoying yourself as you get caught up in the movie.

Such imaginings, such brief and pleasurable flights from reality, more accurately reflect our primal selves than do words; after all, man obviously thought in pictures before he fashioned words to describe his thoughts. Images therefore reach deeply inside us and, because they are both vivid and powerful, involve us more emotionally than do mere words.

As employed in self-hypnosis, images flesh out the syllogistic skeleton. The *modus operandi* is simple. The syllogism provides the framework; then you clothe it with imagery. You picture yourself as you would like to be: strong, confident, self-assured, at ease with yourself and the world around you. If your aim is to be a nonsmoker, you envision yourself in a situation where previously you would have had a cigarette in your mouth or fingers and now are perfectly content without one. If overeating is your problem, you see yourself slender and attractive, happy to reach for a glass of water rather than that piece of chocolate cake. And so on. The purpose for which you're employing self-hypnosis, of course, will dictate the imagery to be used.

As we discuss some of these specific aims, I will suggest the type of imagery that might be appropriate for each. You are encouraged to dream up your own situations, in accordance with your own personality, experience and way of living. I will provide the paradigm; you will reshape it to fit your own needs.

I consider this use of imagery as a complement to the syllogism to be of immense importance. Not only does it give an emotional wallop to the logic of the syllogism, but used alone it offers an alternative to the syllogism. At first, and time permitting, the two are advisedly used consecutively in a two-step implant: the imagery fills out the syllogism. Later on, in the interest of either brevity or variety, you may want to switch back and forth: during one thirty-second exercise engage your unconscious mind just verbally, then, a couple of hours later, just visually. This helps avoid monotony, which could serve as an excuse to give up self-hypnosis before positive results are felt.

Furthermore, focusing on imagery answers the complaint of some people who may object to the intellectual orientation of the syllogism. A few of my patients have said, in effect, "It's too intellectual—give me something I can grab just by feel." Such people may enjoy greater rewards from imagery than from the more cerebral approach of the syllogism.

In sum, I would advise this: begin by including both syllogism and imagery in the self-hypnotic exercise. Let one complement the other. After a fair trial, experiment to determine what feels right for you: to stick with both, to home in on either the verbal or the visual, or to alternate between the two. It will be easier to decide what's best for you after you have become an accomplished self-hypnotist.

Following the self-imagery you may give yourself a post-hypnotic suggestion: an attitude or action you wish to carry over into your everyday life after emerging from your self-hypnosis. If your aim is to be a nonsmoker, you can tell yourself that whenever you feel the desire for a cigarette you will, instead, think of how pleasant and healthful it is to breathe in pure, smoke-free air, to breathe without coughing. Further, you tell yourself that you will feel calm and comfortable and filled with a sense of self-satisfaction for becoming master over your body rather than the reverse.

So, having concentrated on the three elements of the syllogism, engaged in mental imagery and administered a post-hypnotic suggestion, you are now ready to emerge from your self-hypnosis. To do so, count silently backward from three to one:

THREE. Get ready.

TWO. With your eyelids still closed, roll your eyes upward.

ONE. Let your eyelids slowly open.

Now, make tight fists with your hands, then spread your fingers wide and simultaneously yawn.

And that, stripped of hobgoblins and Svengalian trappings, is self-hypnosis.

Again let me caution you: do not be surprised if the experience fails to make the earth move for you. Individual responses vary. You may have a strong and distinct sensation of functioning on an entirely different level from your normal conscious state. At the other extreme, you may simply feel slightly more relaxed as a result of your restful interlude and little more. If so, DON'T BE DISCOURAGED.

Repeat the exercise as often as you can (ideally, every couple of hours), following the directives given here. *Expect* that results will come and *believe* that something is going on in your unconscious mind to work the changes you seek. After all, you have a lot going for you. The suggestions you give yourself are shaped in the form of a syllogism, a cornerstone of logic that has served man well for more than two thousand years. As stated by Aristotle, "A syllogism is a discourse in which, certain things being posited, something else follows from them *by necessity.*" (Italics mine.)

Consider the logic of the three elements of the syllogism as administered during the self-hypnotic exercise.

1. "For my body . . . smoking is a poison."

That is a fact. The Surgeon General of the United States, your own doctor, and even the wrapper on a pack of cigarettes tell you so.

2. "I need my body to live."

Any argument there?

3. "To the degree I want to live, I will protect my body as I would protect [a loved one]."

To live, your body needs care. Cigarettes poison— endanger—your body. You have your choice: you can have either a protected body *or* (not *and*) cigarettes. That is logic, simple and unassailable.

What's more, this method of self-hypnosis for self-help takes an affirmative stand: "Do" rather than "Don't." In breaking the smoking habit, for instance, a person concentrates on the positive action of respecting and protecting his body from the poisons of nicotine and "tar" rather than on the negative injunction: "Don't smoke!" We are conditioned since infancy to respond more favorably to a "Do" than to a "Don't."

A pioneer and teacher of this method, Dr. Herbert Spiegel, has written in *The International Journal of Clinical and Experimental Hypnosis:*

"When the patient accepts the commitment to respect his body, he distracts his attention from the urge to smoke. He now experiences two urges simultaneously—the urge to smoke and the urge to protect his body. By locking them together and emphasizing respect for his body, he concurrently ignores the urge to smoke. Any urge when repeatedly not satisfied and ignored will eventually wither away."

In addition to its emphasis on the affirmative, another great virtue of this method is its brevity. People don't have a lengthy session to prepare for and dread: "I have to go through *that* long thing again." It's over in a few seconds, and therefore one doesn't have the excuse of its length or energy consumption as a way of avoiding the exercise. It's human nature to seek the easy way; so I say, keep it brief and simple. That's compatible with our understanding of the unconscious, too, for it knows no time. Give the unconscious an acceptable idea simply and swiftly.

I have spoken of tailoring the exercise to fit your own personality. Remember, *you* do the hypnotizing. This book gives you the tools and teaches you how to use them. Once you master their use, what you do with them is up to you.

As an example, look at the first line of the syllogism, "For my body, not for me but for my body, smoking is a poison." The word "poison" is a very apt one, especially when linked with smoking. But after a while you may find that another word of your own devising may carry more impact for you. For a medical person, the word "cancer" can be especially meaning-ful. Also, for people who have had a friend or family member who has suffered from the disease, the word "cancer" can provide a kind of shock and thus be quite effective. (I'm assuming it doesn't slip over into having a negative effect, as would happen if the subject diverted his thinking from his problem to his afflicted relative or friend.)

Another word that crops up frequently as a substitute for "poison" is "ruinous." This is a word that can encompass a host of complaints. Excessive drinking can be ruinous. Insomnia can be ruinous. Impotence can be ruinous.

It isn't necessary, or even advisable, to select a word and doggedly cling to it. As for myself, I vary. I use the word "cancer," I use the word "poison," and I also use the word "ruinous." By alternating among the three I find that thinking stays fresh and lively. Choose the metaphor or metaphors you're most comfortable with and that seem to carry the most meaning for you.

The matter of abbreviating or condensing an interpreta-tion, in the case of analysis, or a syllogism in self-hypnosis, is quite a different thing from frequency of practice. Abbreviat-ing the wording can be salutary, if it's comfortable for you, but cutting down on the number of times you hypnotize yourself works the other way and slows results.

I visited my mother recently in the hospital. She had broken her hip, and there had been a couple of operations on it. She endured some pain, as would be expected from such an operation, and I had tried hypnosis with her some months back. When I visited her this time she told me, "You know, I do the exercise every two hours!" And she's in her eighties. Well, that's Mom, but I never feel bashful about encouraging others, as well, to use it every couple of hours—and I don't hear people objecting that it's too much of a burden.

When the problem being assaulted is threatening enough, a person need not hesitate to use the exercise every two to three hours. Then, if a goal is close to achievement, two or three times during the day and *always* at bedtime as part of the ritual for preparing oneself for sound sleep may suffice. You have a powerful technique in your hands, and you want to achieve maximum success with it. Challenge yourself to the fullest to assure that success.

You may wonder why there should be a distinction between "me" and "my body" in the first term of the syllogism, "For my body, not for me but for my body. . . ." The reason is that "your body" isn't "you." The words are not synonymous. You consist of a number of parts, one of which is your body. Your body has to adapt to anything you do to it; it has no choice. This differentiation between the two provides an objectivity, an opportunity to step back and look at your body dispassionately. If you elect to become its keeper and its protector, and offer it the same warmth and concern that you would give a child or anyone close to you, that attitude can then be very beneficial to you.

Now. Let's say you have followed all instructions faithfully. You've relaxed. You've induced the state of self-hypnosis to the best of your ability. You've recited the syllogism with a specific goal in mind. You've done all of these things seven or eight times a day. But nothing seems to be happening. You still have the troubling symptom you want to lose.

This being the case, I have three suggestions that may prove helpful.

(1) There may appear to be no results, but, believe me,

something is going on underneath. Persevere. Keep at it. (2) Examine your motivation and, if warranted, reassess it. (3) Make sure that you're not just reciting the syllogism by rote, rattling the words off like a parrot, without thought and without feeling.

Let's deal with these points in order.

(1) *Persistence.* To engage in this exercise regularly is to achieve results that may not be visible for a while. An airplane moves forward, even if hidden by clouds. It's not hanging stationary inside that cloud bank; you can't see it, but the plane is moving forward. Eventually it will burst out of the clouds into sunlight. Even then, its direction might not always be due north. A depth understanding of the human mind reveals an ebb and flow. Progress tends to be forward, but not continuous: two steps forward, one back; two forward, one back.

(2) *Motivation.* If positive results have not been forthcoming, put your motivation on trial and examine it from two perspectives: to what extent are you willing to give yourself over to the self-hypnotic experience, and how badly do you want to reach your specified goal?

As to the first question, when you engage in the exercise, do you feel that you want to get it over with fast and go on with the business of living, or are you willing to give it your all, your total attention for thirty seconds? There's a world of difference between the two attitudes. A person can do sit-up exercises in the morning so superficially, almost like moving one's forefinger up and down, that there are no results at all. But doing the exercises with full concentration and participation in the same amount of time can make a significant difference.

So it is with hypnosis. Paradoxically, concentration is both the objective and the means of achieving that objective: we're engaging in hypnosis in order to produce greater concentration, but in order to engage in it successfully we must concentrate our attention on it. Paradoxical or not, that's how it works.

The other aspect of motivation, how deeply you *want* to change, spans the range of intensity. A drinking man, say, may sense that his son is losing regard for him as he reels around the house and sees the look of dismay on his son's face. That can add power to his self-suggestion to get rid of his drinking problem. There is a difference of 180 degrees between such a person and one who says, "I'm trying this because my rich uncle wants me to." Such motivation is obviously not reaching his guts, unlike the man who says, "I've got to get over this because I'm losing the respect of my son, and that means more to me than life itself." He's willing to give up his life but not his son's respect; but the two become merged. Result: he's highly motivated. Your motivation need not lead to a life-or-death decision, but it should nonetheless be strong if you want favorable results.

(3) *Feeling.* To guard against the sometimes hollow verbalizing of the syllogism, try varying the wording. We have already suggested alternating among such words as "poison," "cancer" and "ruinous" in the opening term. Then in the third term of the syllogism the subject says to himself, "To the degree that I want to live, I will protect my body [or psychic health or whatever he's working on]." To give that term real power, one should add the name of someone very close.

An example: there was a man whose daughter was in an automobile accident in which her face was badly mangled. He had to keep dabbing the blood away as he waited for the surgeon to get to her. Recalling that wrenching experience brings the intensity of his regard for his daughter vividly home to him and gives the syllogism great impact.

Another example is that of Helen, whom I saw just once. On that visit she presented a weight problem. She weighed two hundred pounds, give or take a few. I instructed her in hypnosis and from then on I was in regular touch with her by telephone. She and her husband traveled a good deal, and she would call from some distant point to let me know how she was progressing. For weight reduction it's helpful for the patient to see an internist, who will recommend a diet. Helen had done so. A diet was devised whereby she would consume five hundred calories a day less than had been her custom, thereby losing a pound a week.

She telephoned me every month or so. Yes, she was losing a pound a week, but it was slow and agonizing. She wondered how she might handle the suffering she endured as she was "starving" herself. Now, there should be no such feeling of starvation if hypnosis is being successful, so something was obviously missing.

She phoned me one day to say that in the midst of her travels, in India, she had seen her grown son. Inquiry revealed that she was worried about the son, who was engaged in a rather hazardous occupation. It struck me that here was a lever that might at once (a) induce motivation and (b) reduce suffering.

From then on she included a thought about her son in her syllogism. In the third step, instead of simply saying, as she had been, "To the degree that I want to live, I will protect my body," she added, "as I would protect my son."

She reported in a phone call that her recent diminished food intake had not been accompanied by a feeling of suffering.

I should point out that although such a coda should have been included in her exercise from the beginning, it had not been. Whether I had failed to emphasize it sufficiently during her visit to me or whether she had simply forgotten about it, I cannot say. The point is that this addition to her motivation gave emotional clout to her self-suggestion about weight control. I suggested that she could further meditate upon the matter, reminding herself of feelings she had about her son and his safety, and ask herself why she should not give the same consideration and protection to her own body that she so freely gave to the safety of her son. At last report, she was within twenty pounds of her goal.

So let me underline the desirability of checking to see whether one is just uttering words while omitting both thought and feeling.

We're really dealing with two concepts in this self-hypnotic exercise of ours: cold syllogistic logic mixed with warm subjective emotion. When filtered through the unconscious, the distillate is heady stuff, indeed.

Certainly while learning self-hypnosis you will engage in a muscle-relaxing exercise before the induction. Once you have mastered the self-hypnotic technique you may choose to eliminate the preliminary muscle-relaxing and thus be able to complete a session in thirty seconds.

I recommend that you reread the instructions earlier in this chapter for inducing both relaxation and the hypnotic state itself, and practice them until you are comfortable with their use. You may even want to put the instructions on tape and play them back until you have thoroughly absorbed the technique.

In the remaining chapters of this book, we will try to discuss just about any purpose for which you may wish to employ self-hypnosis. Undoubtedly there will be some we have not anticipated. If that is the case with you, simply turn to the chapter under which the difficulty or desired change most logically would fall (*e.g.,* "how to break Unwanted Habits" or "Sharpening Skills of Mind and Body"), find a listing that approximates the one you're looking for, and alter the wording and imagery to fit your purpose.

Instructions are tailored to meet specific needs. I suggest you follow these directions until you are sure you have mastered the technique before experimenting with the wording of the syllogism and/or the subsequent imagery.

I recommend now that rather than skipping to the discussion that interests you most, you read straight through, *then* flip back to the subject of special concern. By so doing you will (1) gain a deeper understanding of the nature of self-hypnosis and its wide-ranging efficacy, and (2) perhaps get some ideas for correcting problems or improving performance in areas that for one reason or another might not occur to you otherwise.

And now, primed in the theory and technique of self-hypnosis, you should be ready to put into practice what we've been teaching. Let us begin by learning to eliminate the negative.

CHAPTER 6

How to Break Unwanted Habits

Most of our days, fortunately, have a kind of "groove" to them. Actions that require little thought and planning to execute are performed almost by rote, automatically. If this were not the case, our lives would become tediously complex and we would spend much of our time thinking about how to tie our shoes, prepare our meals, get to work, and so on. As it is, we can carry out the routine chores of daily living with next to no thought, allowing us to turn our attention to more demanding and rewarding activities. The repetitive tasks of life become habits—*wanted* habits.

But habits can also be *unwanted,* and these groove just as deeply into the pattern of our days. They work against us as they waste our time. If after arising in the morning, say, we know we have a limited amount of time to get to work and, on the way to breakfast, we notice the morning paper lying on the table, pick it up and habitually spend the next hour engrossed in the daily news, then chances are we'd spend a good share of our remaining time explaining our tardiness or, more likely, looking for a new job.

In our discussion of habits, incidentally, we will term them either "wanted" or "unwanted" rather than "good" or "bad." The words "good" and "bad" carry a moral connotation: they signify a certain judgment. In the example cited in the paragraph above, reading a newspaper is not "bad" in a moral sense, but it is definitely unwanted at that particular time.

"Wanted" and "unwanted" are "ego" words, implying a self-determined rather than an externally judged choice. Just as in psychoanalysis, our aim here is to shove material out of the "conscience" camp and into the "ego" arena, where an individual can get a better grip on it.

Quite often, we might even say usually, ridding yourself of an unwanted habit demands more than simple choice. You may consciously want to drop the habit, but translating the wish into action is another matter entirely. This is so for a couple of reasons. In the first place, a habit, by its very nature and definition, is so ingrained in a person's way of behaving that it is done reflexively, even without thought. So merely thinking "I won't do thus-and-so" doesn't necessarily touch us deeply enough to arrest undesired behavior.

Furthermore, the longer a habit has been with us and the more often it has been performed, the more firmly it is entrenched and the more difficult to dispel. Take smoking. It isn't rare to see an individual light up a second cigarette when he already has one burning in an ashtray or when he is engrossed in a conversation or task, totally unaware that he's doing so. Such actions, hammered into an individual's behavior pattern dozens of times daily, day in and decade out, become second nature, become in fact almost as natural as breathing (which becomes, ironically, harder and harder for the smoker to do).

In fact, there are even physical—neurological—underpinnings for such habits. The nerve pathways in our bodies might be compared to dirt roadways. Before any vehicle passes over a dirt roadway, that road is smooth. When an automobile goes down the road for the first time, its tires leave marks, but the ruts are shallow—rain or wind can easily erase them and make the road smooth again. But after a hundred trips, with the tires grooving in time and time again, deeper and deeper, rain or wind will make little impression on the deep ruts. They'll stay there.

The same can be said of people. To stretch the metaphor a bit, we're born with smooth roadways in our brains. When a small child first tries to button his jacket or to tie his shoes, the effort is fumbling and clumsy and fraught with frustration. Many more tries are called for until the child gets the hang of it and the successful sequence of movements comes to be grooved into a behavior pattern.

Physiologically, the instructions for these movements travel on nerve pathways to the muscles and back again. The message is sent along the *afferent* pathway to the central nervous system, *e.g.,* "I want to lift my foot." The impulse continues on the *efferent* pathway from the central nervous system to the muscle: "Lift the foot." After a while such messages, reinforced through countless repetitions, are transmitted automatically and with electric rapidity.

Back to the car and roadway. Suppose the car decides to avoid the well-worn grooves and cut a new path; what happens? There's a tendency for the car to slide right back into the old grooves. Just so with people trying to get out of the rut of old habits: they have a tendency to slide back into their old ways.

Still, we're not born with unwanted habits. We learn them and we can unlearn them. They're *conditioned reflexes;* we can *un*condition them. And here is where self-hypnosis steps in to give the individual a boost up out of the ruts of established habits and onto a smooth pathway of new behavior.

The advantage it offers over the trial and error of simple willpower derives from the raised state of consciousness that characterizes the state of self-hypnosis. Being a neurological phenomenon in itself, this raised state of consciousness appears to lift the individual above former behavior patterns. To extend the dirt-roadway analogy still further, it's now like being in a hovercraft skimming a few inches above the road, up over the ruts—that is, above the habits.

Whatever the habit you want to work on, the induction process is precisely the same: only the verbal implants and the subsequent imagery will vary.

To capsulize the induction process: at the count of ONE you will do one thing, at the count of TWO, two things, and at the count of THREE, three things:

ONE. Roll your eyes up toward the top of your head, as high as you can get them.

TWO. Still staring upward, slowly close your eyes and take a deep breath.

THREE. Exhale, let your eyes relax, and let your body float.

Then you will spend a moment, or more if time permits, picturing yourself at a pleasant site where you feel most comfortable and at peace.

Now, as you continue to float down deeper and deeper into that chair you're resting in, you feel a bit removed from your body—an object distinct from you. Because it is a thing apart from you, you can give it instructions as to how you wish it to act.

At this point, the specific purpose for your self-hypnosis will determine the wording of the syllogism and the content of the imagery. We offer suggestions in the discussions of various habits, which you may either follow as presented or revise as you see fit.

Smoking

Rather than identify all of the demons that the act of smoking calls up, let us assume that you are well aware of the dangers and the harm inherent in the practice. The very fact that you're prepared to use self-hypnosis to help you stop smoking demonstrates that you possess perhaps *the* most essential prerequisite to dropping the habit: motivation.

In *A Single-Treatment Method to Stop Smoking Using Ancillary Self-Hypnosis,* Dr. Herbert Spiegel makes the essential point that an individual who engages in self-hypnosis does it voluntarily. "The lack of coercion," he writes, "acts as a screening device to rule out all those who are not sufficiently motivated."

Relaxation, the step preparatory to engaging in self-hypnosis, plays two roles in regard to smoking (and also with other so-called nervous habits). Many people claim that nervousness is the reason they smoke, that smoking calms them down. If this were true, we might expect the person who always seems to have a cigarette in his mouth or between his fingers to be a very placid individual, for he's "calming" himself almost constantly.

But just the opposite is likely to be the case: the heavy smoker tends to be quite a nervous person. Thus, the tail wags the dog; since nicotine actually exacerbates nervous tension, the heavy smoker is nervous in part at least because he smokes so much. So relaxation, while performing its primary job of facilitating the induction process, will by its very nature diminish the tension that many people say drives them to smoke.

Here, then, are the steps to follow in using self-hypnosis to stop smoking.

Begin by making yourself relaxed and imagining yourself perfectly at peace in some tranquil setting. Next, induce the state of self-hypnosis. You now feel slightly removed from your body, the outer shell that encompasses you. Mentally give that body the following instructions:

"For my body, not for me but for my body, smoking is a poison.

"I need my body to live.

"To the degree I want to live, I will protect my body as I would protect [name of a loved one]."

Now for the imagery. Imagine yourself in situations where heretofore you would have been inclined to smoke, first in the company of other people and then alone. Picture yourself in that social situation, in a room surrounded by others. The room is completely free of smoke. The air is clear and pleasant, and one can take a deep, refreshing breath without coughing. You feel very comfortable, happy and relaxed, as you sit there smiling, breathing freely and easily.

Now imagine yourself alone, perhaps writing a letter or watching television. You're quite content not to have anything in your fingers or mouth. You're simply concentrating on that letter or TV screen and enjoying the breathing in of clean, fresh air.

You may now tell yourself that if at any time between emerging from this self-hypnotic experience and engaging in the next exercise you should find yourself longing for a cigarette, you will instead recall the picture of that room filled with pure, health-restoring, smoke-free air. How pleasant and relaxed and comfortable you felt just being there and knowing that this is how you can feel from now on. What's more, there's a sudden surge of pride as you recognize that you are once again in control of yourself—you, not your habit, now call the shots.

Then you emerge from your self-hypnotic exercise. With eyes still closed, count silently backward from three to one:

THREE. Get ready.

TWO. With lids closed, roll your eyes upward.

ONE. Let your eyelids slowly open. Make tight fists of your hands, then spread your fingers wide, and simultaneously yawn.

Drinking

I observe that when I treat patients for overdrinking, the matter is virtually a duplication of smoking: both habits involve a wish for oral gratification, both carry the seeds of self-destruction, and both are used ostensibly to help the person "relieve nervous tension" or "feel better."

I say "ostensibly" feel better because, in fact, both practices are apt to do just the opposite, by attacking such body parts as the heart, lungs, liver, circulation and brain, and certainly in the case of drinking, if less so in smoking, the habit erodes one's self-respect and endangers relationships with family, friends and fellow workers.

The traditionalist may object to the removal of the symptom—overdrinking—without getting at the root cause of the overindulgence. To this I say, "I agree; let's find out the reason. But let's put out the fire that's burning down the house before we try to determine how it got started."

By way of example I'd like to tell you about Susie. Susie was a 35-year-old homemaker sent to me by her pastor because of her drinking problem. Her husband was a traveling man, away from home for at least three days and nights every week. I saw Susie only twice concerning this matter. On her first visit she explained that she found her husband's absences almost unendurable, and so she would ease her loneliness with alcohol. This would get her into trouble, because when her husband returned home after his weekly trips he would find her intoxicated.

Susie said that she was "unable" to hide her drinking from her husband. (In fact, there was the possibility she might have been getting intoxicated to show him how she felt about things and to force him to stay at home.) At any rate, she simply told me that drinking was her way of handling the problem and, further, that she did not want to be psychoanalyzed. I offered her hypnosis, but she wanted no part of that, either. She left me with the request that I persuade her husband to rearrange his schedule so he'd be home more of the time.

I did speak to her husband, who said he'd been approved for a change in work assignment, but that it wouldn't go into effect for three months. Susie heard about the change and was overjoyed. When her husband returned home three days later, he found her intoxicated. The same thing occurred the following week and the week after that. In other words the information that her husband would soon be adjusting his work schedule was not keeping this woman sober. Her husband was reporting this to me by telephone, while urging Susie to keep coming to me. She declined, but she finally did return after the third week.

Her husband, disillusioned and fearing she would not keep her resolution to stop drinking after he started his new schedule, phoned me before she came in. I should feel free, he informed me, to tell Susie that if she were unable to handle the problem, he would leave her.

Susie and I talked for a few minutes at the beginning of the session without my mentioning her husband's call. I advised a regular treatment program. She thanked me just the same, but no thanks. I then took her husband's suggestion and told her that, unless she got into some curative plan to help her master this problem, he had decided to leave her. She listened quietly in her own gentle way, said she was surprised to learn this and thought she'd go now. Which she did.

A week later I had a phone call from her husband, thanking me for "curing" her. He had come home this week, he explained, to find Susie in good condition and with no signs of alcohol in the house. Puzzled, I asked him to keep me informed.

The following week he gave me the same report. I asked him to put Susie on the phone. She informed me that she had had no desire to drink since our last session, adding, "Your hypnosis certainly worked." I asked her to tell me what she could recall about the "hypnosis." She replied that she couldn't remember very much about the session, just that during the "hypnosis" I'd said her husband was very distressed with her drinking and that he hoped with all his heart she would take steps to stop it. She said nothing about his possibly leaving her.

That was the last time I have been in direct contact with the couple. I understand from others who have come in, referred by these people, that Susie has not had a drop of alcohol since.

Obviously hers was a case of spontaneous self-hypnosis, since I never did hypnotize her. Like spontaneous combustion, it happened without anyone doing anything to induce the condition.

An interesting sidelight to Susie's experience was her amnesia concerning the bad news I had delivered to her during the session; she simply chose to forget it because the news was so unthinkable. Amnesia is not unusual in hypnosis, but it usually follows another person's—a hypnotist's—suggestion that the subject will experience amnesia regarding the experience after he emerges from the state.

I offer this case as an unusual instance of self-induced hypnosis without formal induction. Had Susie allowed me to teach her the technique of self-hypnosis, the means would have been slightly different, because she would have consciously induced the state, but I am confident that the results would have been identical. Hypnosis occurred spontaneously with Susie because of such powerful and dramatic motivation: her husband, whom she deeply loved, would leave her if she didn't do something about her problem fast. She was just about to hit bottom.

Sadly, many problem drinkers do not find the motivation to do something about their plight until they actually do hit bottom, be the problem a desperate home situation, lost livelihood or some other personal calamity. Our hope here is to offer, through self-hypnosis, the means whereby the problem drinker can get his own life under control and avoid doing irreparable damage both to himself and to those he treasures most.

Let me hasten to say that in suggesting self-hypnosis, I have no wish to compete with Alcoholics Anonymous. Although self-hypnosis can definitely relieve the problem, for the average problem drinker neither hypnosis nor psychoanalysis nor any other individual therapy I know can hold a candle to AA. There's something about AA—the dedication, the group fellowship, the mutual support that AA offers people who overdrink—that usually proves more effective than either self-hypnosis as practiced by an individual or the one-to-one relationship of psychotherapist and patient. (Ideally, the alcoholic sees a therapist *and* joins AA.)

But that said, there is nothing to prevent us from borrowing some of the successful elements of AA for our work here. One such component is the concept of sobriety. An AA member will congratulate himself: "I lost my job, my wife kicked me out and my children won't talk to me. But at least I have my sobriety now; that's a possession of which I'm very proud."

Another useful AA concept is *a day at a time:* "Tomorrow I can get drunk, but today . . . thanks just the same." It's a kind of merciful procrastination, always putting off until tomorrow the drunk you could have engaged in today.

How does all of this relate to self-hypnosis as practiced for overindulgence? Simply that it provides us with a rich source of material for the implants one administers after the induction. As mentioned earlier, the self-hypnosis procedures for smoking and drinking are quite similar up until the imagery part of the implant. First comes the relaxation exercise, followed by induction of the hypnotic state and recitation of the syllogism, during which the word "alcohol" is substituted for "smoking":

"For my body, not for me but for my body, alcohol is a poison.

"I need my body to live.

"To the degree I want to live, I will protect my body as I would protect ———."

Now, the imagery implant. The individual confronting his drinking problem imagines a screen up on the wall on which are played out scenes of his own invention. For instance, he may picture a social situation where it has been his custom to drink liberally. But now, in his mind's eye, he sees himself on the screen smiling and at ease as the waiter or hostess approaches to ask what he'd like to drink. "What I'd really like," he responds, "is a plain tonic with a slice of lime." As people look at him strangely because it has previously been his wont to order a triple martini, he smiles back and remarks, "Well, that's the way I happen to feel at the moment."

He visualizes himself circulating through the group, glass of tonic in hand, and reflects to himself, "I don't care whether the people around me know I have plain tonic. This is what I'm choosing to drink. I like it; I'm comfortable with it. I see that other people are getting loud and tipsy and slurring their speech. That's their problem; thank heaven I'm not so inclined." He sees himself moving about, head held high and feeling strong, comfortable and proud of himself.

Another person, let's say a woman, may similarly picture herself in a restaurant. She tells the waiter, "Make mine ginger ale, please." It's really no one else's business why she orders ginger ale, but if someone wants to know, "How come you're not . . . ," she feels quite comfortable responding, "That's just what I feel like today."

Furthermore, wherever she is—in someone's home, in a bar or restaurant, or at a convention—it feels good to be holding a glass filled with something that won't poison her body. She might think to herself at such a time, "I am showing regard and respect for and caring for my body, this envelope in which I have my being. I feel very proud of what I'm doing, and I'm grateful for my sobriety."

As with smoking, the person with a drinking problem is also encouraged to envision himself alone, as well as in a group situation, and to tailor the imagery to conform with his own habits. I'm thinking of a person with the perilous habit of pulling out a bottle while driving, and guzzling as he weaved in and out of traffic. How he ever got to my office without destroying himself en route is a mystery.

Such a person would visualize himself driving along quite comfortably and enjoyably, perhaps listening to the radio or just observing the countryside, and saying to himself in a self-congratulatory manner, "I feel happy avoiding my old skull and crossbones. How good it feels to engage in easy, effortless sobriety—a day at a time." Your own setting, it is hoped, would be different from that of the tippling driver, though the visual implant might be similar.

After engaging in the imagery, you bring yourself out of self-hypnosis in the customary three-step manner:

THREE. Get ready.

TWO. Keeping lids closed, roll your eyes upward.

ONE. Slowly open your lids. Then, make tight fists of your hands, spread your fingers wide and yawn.

Since we're dealing with overdrinking, a word might be said about overindulgence in nonalcoholic beverages as well. Probably the greatest offender here is coffee, although such beverages as tea, Coke, Pepsi or even milk can also cause problems. Some people, in office situations, for example, complain that coffee is so readily available that they find themselves swilling it down, then suffering the jitters along with acidic stomachs. They read that caffeine, acids and other poisons in coffee can also give them aches and pains and even shorten their lives.

The self-hypnotic prescription for abstinence, or at least to reduce consumption, is the same for nonalcoholic as for alcoholic beverages. First the syllogism, along these lines:

"I'm made up of a number of components, one of the most vital of which is my body; the overdrinking of coffee is dangerous for that body.

"I need my body to live. This body is the framework in which I have my being, and I need it to survive.

"To the degree I *choose* to survive, I will preserve and protect my body as I would protect ————."

The substitution of water for harmful beverages in the subsequent visualizing can be especially effective. Some experts in internal medicine urge people to drink eight glasses of water a day. What a wonderful opportunity here not only to abstain from poisonous fluids like coffee, tea or cola, but at the same time to realize the benefits of water. If eight cups of coffee a day will shorten your life, while on the other hand eight glasses of water a day will lengthen it, by abstaining from one and adopting the other we enjoy a double gain.

When visualizing this, picture yourself going to the faucet, letting the water splash out for a moment or so, and then pouring yourself a glassful of the cool, crystal-clear liquid. Or picture filling a large pitcher with water, putting it on ice and going to the refrigerator to pour yourself a glass whenever the whistle wants wetting. At the office, see yourself walking over to the water cooler rather than to that ever-present coffee container, and treating yourself to a drink of pure water, free of coloring, preservatives, flavors or artificial anything.

If you're with others and someone asks, "How about a cup of coffee?" imagine yourself saying, "Thanks, just water for me, if you would." Then you take the glass contentedly and slowly sip that cooling and refreshing liquid while congratulating yourself for protecting your health.

Finally, after emerging from your self-hypnosis, why not celebrate your new self-mastery by quaffing a glassful of clear H_2O?

Overeating

We are a prosperous nation overall, with plenty of food at our disposal. Most of us (with some glaring and lamentable exceptions) have enough money to insure that we are comfortably overfed. As a consequence, so many of us suffer from overweight that the reducing business is big business: pill producers, diet devisers and exercise studios never seem at a loss for customers who claim they want to shed poundage.

It has been said that inside every fat person there's a thin one struggling to get out. Alas, in all too many cases, the thin man spends a lifetime trying and still never makes good his escape. Despite the image of the jolly fat man, hardly anyone enjoys being overweight—it makes most people miserable, not infrequently to the point of virtually ruining their lives because of self-consciousness and shattered confidence. Obesity just seems to sneak up on some of us, and by the time we realize it, overeating or eating the wrong foods has, like the excess poundage itself, become a painfully hard habit to lose.

Self-hypnosis, I submit, can help that thin man wriggle free of his shackles of "too too solid flesh" and begin a new life. A paper in *The International Journal of Clinical and Experimental Hypnosis* (January 1975) reports on such a case. In their survey of hypnosis in medical and dental practice, Sidney E. and Mitchell P. Pulver quote one family physician:

> About a year and a half ago, I had a patient come to my office. She had been to many doctors in an effort to reduce. She said that because of her extreme obesity she hardly ever stepped out of the house, that she was gloomy and really avoided people. She came in weighing some 380 pounds, and I induced a trance in the first session and concentrated on telling her that she would follow her diet and find that as she lost weight she really liked people. She came in weekly for the first three or four sessions, after which I began to teach her self-hypnosis. Well, this lady lost 150 pounds in all, but more than that, she became a different person. Going from practically an introvert and hardly ever getting out of

the house, she got enough courage to get a part-time job selling cosmetics. She would arrange to have parties to show the cosmetics and would use self-hypnosis before the party. She became the number two salesperson in the state and made literally tens of thousands of dollars that year.

In brief, here is the therapy to follow in using self-hypnosis for weight control. After inducing the self-hypnotic state, mentally recite the syllogism:

"For my body, not for me but for my body, overeating or the eating of wrong foods is ruinous.

"I need my body to live.

"To the degree I want to live, I will preserve and protect my body as I would protect ————."

For the attendant imagery the individual may picture himself in the two situations where he is likely to overdo his eating: between meals and at the dinner table. With his eyes closed, he envisions a movie screen on the wall. He himself is up on that screen, reading, chatting with others, watching television, or in whatever context he finds himself when he gets himself into trouble calorically.

Instead of reaching for the popcorn, potato chips or peanuts as he previously would have done, he now sees himself simply concentrating on the conversation, television screen or printed page, and congratulating himself for feeling comfortable with nothing on the table except perhaps a glass of water.

A second scene one may conjure up is the dinner table. Inclined to reach for that second slice of bread? Instead, bring your hand to your forehead and remind yourself: "Protect my body." Look at the cake, bread, potatoes or pie and let the thought occur: "That's for someone else. I've had enough." Put down your fork, breathe deeply and allow a sense of pride at having been content with a single helping to course through your body.

You may then wish to picture yourself engaging in a very simple but effective exercise: simply put your hands on the edge of the table and push. Even better, at that point you rise from your chair and walk away from the table.

Another bit of imagery I would urge on the self-hypnotist is this: when you picture yourself on that imaginary movie screen, see yourself as being slim. Give yourself the ideal lines that you have seen on others and that you'd love to see on yourself. Cut that stomach line and hip line down to the proportions you want. Take an imaginary black crayon and outline the whole figure, making the lines sharp and firm. Hold that image. To the extent that you can hold that picture of slimness, you will become thin.

And then bring yourself out of your self-hypnosis, repeating it routinely every couple of hours. The exercise can be especially useful at times of temptation, to be engaged in as a pleasant, no-calorie substitute for a fattening snack or an extra helping at meals. Just before dinner would be a fine time to practice it.

As a postscript to this discussion, I'd like to mention one of my patients, "Mr. Happiness." (He has this name in my ruminations because he has often told me, "All I want out of life is to be happy.")

Mr. Happiness and I have seen a lot of problems through together, including the suicide of his sister, a heart attack, the breakup of his former business and the forming of a new one; but now, I'm glad to say, he's a happily retired man. He drops in every six to eight weeks just "to keep the wheels oiled," as he says.

Shortly after I had become familiar with hypnotherapy, I told him about it with some enthusiasm and invited him to use it in the handling of a current problem. He demurred; he was afraid of it. Some time went by, and during this period I wrote a little pamphlet on hypnosis. One day I gave Mr. Happiness a copy. He came in some weeks later to say, "Gee, that's interesting stuff. It sure isn't psychoanalysis, but you say all you do is . . ." and he repeated the steps of the induction process.

"Yes," I replied, "it's just a simple one-two-three thing. Are you sure you don't want to try it?"

Again he declined: "Oh, boy, not me!"

The subject was not brought up again for several months. I should mention that Mr. Happiness was a portly man and, particularly because of his heart attack, had been instructed to keep his weight down. But what a struggle: those potatoes, those rich desserts and those knishes! Then one day he said to me, "You know, I've been doing something lately that I thought you'd be interested in. When I go to bed at night I just count to three and say to myself, 'In the morning I will eat nothing and drink only grapefruit juice but still feel well filled. I'll go out into the air and take a deep breath, and the world will seem good and I won't need any more food.'" (Note this patient's abridgment of the induction to the brief: "I just count to three.")

He then confessed to me that he had been doing this for the past few months, that he had lost weight and was feeling quite comfortable doing so. Yet he didn't want me to hypnotize him.

That, of course, is the beauty of self-hypnosis. He didn't have to be hypnotized; he could and did hypnotize himself to accomplish what he wanted. You can do the same.

Drugs

As with smoking, there is little point in dwelling on the harmful effects of drugs. To understate the case, drugs do not enhance your health. They may well destroy it; they may well destroy you.

Yet people take drugs. They want to change the way they feel: they want to perk up and they want to calm down. I have no quarrel with trying to change how you feel *if* you can do so without endangering mind and body, which of course is just what drugs do. The technique we're offering in this book accomplishes the same end as drugs—an altered state of consciousness—and with no risk, but with certain benefit.

If a person's drug problem has not reached the point of physical addiction, then the self-hypnotic exercise can well serve as a substitute when the need for a change of spirits is felt.

In the syllogism he may use any number of appropriate words to describe the consequences of drugs:

"For my body, not for me but for my body, drugs are a poison [or "ruinous," "deadly," "crippling," "cancerous," etc.].

"I need my body to live.

"To the degree I want to live, I will protect my body as I would protect ———."

Then on your imaginary movie screen you may picture yourself moving about your room. You can see, as you watch yourself, that you have an urge, a wish to swallow, smoke or sniff something that will alter your state of consciousness and make you feel better. You're feeling kind of low and want to brighten things up.

So you watch yourself on that screen and you see that *you*, not drugs, can make that happen. You are your body's master. You tell it to be calm and it obeys. You tell it to be content. It obeys. You tell it to be happy and you see yourself on the screen smiling and possessed of an overwhelming feeling of peace of mind; all is well with you and the world around you. You can make your body feel any way you want it to feel.

You may then add the posthypnotic suggestion that when you emerge from the hypnotic state you will feel calm, relaxed, buoyant. And should you at any time feel the urge to alter your mood, you will find yourself thinking of a scene of joy or tranquillity, and your mood will shift accordingly.

Procrastination

Here's a real gem. Who among us can claim to be guiltless of putting off till tomorrow what might have been done yesterday? Certainly not I, and I'd wager not you, either. Tempting matters, as urgent as they are interesting, seem to materialize to overwhelm the best of our intentions; procrastination wins the war before we get around to starting the battle.

The trick in grappling with procrastination is to make what is useful to the self more attractive than any other option at the moment. Here again, self-hypnosis steps in to lend a hand with so universal a problem.

How do we tackle it? First, the syllogism. The habit of putting things off results in setbacks on two counts: the loss of our self-regard by not letting us feel in charge of our own lives, and also the loss of other people's regard for us, how they feel about us. If the latter occurs in a job situation, procrastination can mean the loss of a promotion or even of the job itself. In friendship, postponing letters or engagements can mean losing friends.

The exact nature of losses caused by procrastination is highly individual and depends on circumstances, but by and large, most of the things we put off affect us in one of three basic areas of our lives—career, family and friendship—as well as being injurious to our self-esteem. In constructing the syllogism for his own particular situation, the procrastinator may link the elements of his feelings of self-worth with his relationships with others in one of the three categories just mentioned. For instance, a person who postpones doing chores around the house may think:

"For my self-satisfaction and for my family relationships, to put off household chores is ruinous.

"I need my self-satisfaction and my family love in order to live contentedly.

"So, to the extent I wish to live contentedly, I will act promptly."

Or the procrastinating secretary may recite:

"For my own self-regard and for the respect of [her boss], putting off my tasks is disastrous.

"I need my self-regard and the respect of ———— to live happily.

"To the degree I wish to live happily, I will insure my own feelings of self-regard and the respect of ———— by doing things promptly."

The subsequent imagery can then be made vivid and forceful. Let's consider the man who has some repairs to make about the house. For example, there may be a bit of linoleum sticking up on the kitchen floor that someone might trip over, and his wife has asked him repeatedly to fix it. He can either ignore the difficulty and let it fester—both in his mind and on the floor—or, and here begins the movie on that imaginary screen on the wall, he can do something about it.

He may see himself getting out the implements he needs to mend the thing, proceed with the steps that result in correcting the hazard and now, with the flap of linoleum securely in place, stand back with an expression of satisfaction on his face—along with a peck on the cheek from his pleased wife. He not only has accomplished something concrete that makes *him* feel good, but has also furthered his *family* good feeling.

The same approach may be employed by the woman faced with cleaning up her dishes after a big dinner or a party. She watches herself do so, on that imaginary movie screen, with feelings of satisfaction over her swift performance of the job, followed by expressions of admiration and appreciation from her husband as she finishes.

Similarly, at the office, envision yourself returning to work after a coffee break. The girl at the next desk wants to chat with you. Visualize the work appearing more and more inviting. Irresistibly, you turn readily to the task at hand, accomplish it easily, *then* take a few minutes off to talk with the friend.

Such scenes can be multiplied a thousand times over.

Let's look at still another setting: school. I think of a chap who roomed down the hall from me while I was an undergraduate at Dartmouth College. I observed that on weekends this fellow never studied. I marveled at this, and one day I asked him about it. "Did you ever notice," he replied, "that after three o'clock on weekday afternoons I'm hammering away at my books?" The rest of us never noticed that, because those were the hours we would be out playing touch football or otherwise nonacademically engaged. My friend down the hall was getting his work done early in order to have the weekends free to go down to Boston or over to Smith College. The procrastinators spent Sunday nights boning up, and woke up bleary-eyed on Monday morning.

All right, so what shall you—one of the procrastinators—do? Answer: self-hypnotize and visualize! During self-

hypnosis, see all other options as less compelling than immediately tending to the work. Picture yourself arriving at
your room from class and facing all of those temptations: the
telephone call to the girl friend, the roommate who wants to
play a game of cards, that sexy magazine lying on the chair.

See yourself on the screen, passing up the telephone, thanking the roommate, saying, "This bit of study for tomorrow is
important to me right now," and turning away from the magazine. Everything else in the room seems pale and insignificant
when compared to the attractiveness of those studies. Watch
yourself sit down, turn eagerly to the work at hand and read
with great interest and concentration, thankful that you have
the strength to perform this act without strain and with a
feeling of comfort and gratification.

On the other side of the ledger we have the procrastinating
professor. I have a patient with such a problem. He postpones
two things: the reading and correcting of papers his students
write and his own writing of reports for the dean on his
students' semester work.

At the close of his teaching day, he remains in school for
brief self-hypnosis. His self-hypnotic visualizing takes the
form of seeing himself arriving home an hour later, taking off
his coat and gazing about the room. A table is piled high with
newspapers and magazines and other enticing reading matter,
while over there his bed beckons for a refreshing nap. But
today he also has those reports to write for the dean. On the
screen he "sees" his mind suddenly flood with a realization of
how good it will feel to have those reports finished and behind
him. He watches himself cross to his desk, sit down and begin
to write the reports. He swiftly finishes one, puts it aside,
reaches for another, finishes that one, goes on to another, and
so on until he's done.

The scene changes to the dean's office, where my patient
turns the reports over to the dean and gets a handshake and a
"Well done!" As he comes out of the office he notices two or
three of his students who spot him and express their gratitude
that he's helping them further their careers by getting the

reports in on time. His self-treatment concluded, my professor can now leave school, armed for an evening of victory over procrastination.

Another man, a concert pianist, came to me seeking treatment for depression, but it developed that he also had a problem with procrastination, which if ignored would surely have hampered his career. As he reported to me, "I'd rather watch *I Love Lucy* than practice the mazurka, and I'd rather practice the mazurka than practice my scales." So there was a hierarchy of avoidance, wherein he would postpone what was useful, profitable and designed to further his career, in the name of something that was immediately more fun.

For that one, again go to the picture on the wall. Let's say you're a pianist and you're to practice two hours tomorrow morning. Take a few minutes tonight to hypnotize yourself and imprint that picture in detail. See yourself rising from the breakfast table and facing a choice. Should you lounge around with the morning newspaper and the magazines there on the sofa that are so alluring, or should you go directly to the piano? You watch yourself gazing from one to the other. You observe an expression of distaste cross your face as you consider the first alternative, then you see yourself, smiling now, move firmly and resolutely toward the piano.

Watch yourself sit down and once again face a choice: Beethoven's Sonata #8 is there on one side of the music stand, and the scales are on the other. The sonata is very tempting compared with the scales, but observe yourself moving eagerly toward that which is most useful to you. You start with the scales. See yourself gratified at doing what you know is really in your own best interest. Finally, watch yourself turn from the scales when you are done with them, and begin to play the sonata. After giving yourself the posthypnotic suggestion that tomorrow's piano playing will go according to plan, emerge from self-hypnosis.

I've gone on at some length in order to show how visual implants may be concocted for any conceivable problem in procrastination. This imagery, of course, fits into the standard framework of self-hypnosis: preliminary relaxation, induction of the self-hypnotic state, syllogism, visual implant, posthypnotic suggestion, and emergence from the state.

And now, without a moment's procrastination, we move to the final subject of this chapter.

Stuttering, Nail Biting and Other Nervous Habits

Stuttering is a subject of some personal interest to me, since I did my doctoral dissertation at the University of Michigan on the personality characteristics of stutterers. I had been motivated in this direction by my father, himself a stutterer, who assisted in the research. As a boy, Father attended a speech clinic in Cleveland, where therapists had instructed him to tap out a beat with his fingers as he talked, just as one would drum on a table.

This practice is in consonance with the old observation that the habitual stutterer ceases stuttering when he breaks into song. The conclusion to be drawn is that easy, fluid speech, like music, is built on a foundation of rhythm, tempo and beat. A smooth speaker is following the natural beat of his body, the regular and dependable beat of his heart. We follow this pulsating rhythm unconsciously when our speech is smooth. When we get bogged down and stammer, we're violating this natural body beat.

To help cure his affliction, the stutterer needs to learn to accommodate himself to his internal beat. In the process, he may use an external bit of apparatus for a while, a metronome. The individual sets the metronome at whatever beat seems comfortable, then practices speaking in the rhythm and at the rate of the metronome's beat:

"I-am-speak-ing-ac-cord-ing-to-the-beat-of-the-met-ro-nome." He does this every two or three hours until he gets accustomed to speaking at a pace in harmony with his natural body beat. At times he may find it inconvenient or conspicuous, or both, to carry his metronome around to practice with;

under such circumstances he may simply tap his foot at the same beat he found most comfortable when using the metronome.

The metronome offers a practical approach to conquering the problem of stuttering. But we also find the concept of the metronomic beat quite compatible with self-hypnosis. In practice, the stutterer follows the usual self-hypnotic approach: the syllogism and then imagery. Since stuttering carries a twofold liability—for the stutterer himself and for his listeners—the syllogism may be worded to cover both:

"For my feelings of self-worth and for the regard of people I communicate with, stuttering is a ruinous barrier.

"I need my own feelings of self-worth and the regard of others in order to live in comfort.

"To the degree I wish to live in comfort, I will speak smoothly."

Then the imagery. Picture yourself on that white screen we've been talking about. You see yourself pick up a metronome, set it at a beat you like and be-gin-speak-ing-at-an-eas-y-rate,-the-words-flow-ing-smooth-ly-and-ef-fort-less-ly.

Next, imagine yourself bursting into song. The lyrics pour out crystal-clear, without strain. When you finish, you see yourself turning to a companion and finding your speech has the same easy flow that was evident during the singing. Your companion exclaims, "Great! You sang that song so smoothly, so easily, so ably, without a hitch." He shakes your hand, claps you on the shoulder and congratulates you: "Your speech is just as smooth as your singing."

Finally, you may give yourself a posthypnotic suggestion: "When I emerge from this state, I will find that I can continue this same easy, rhythmic flow of speech just as if the metronome were still ticking." And in a sense, it is.

You then conclude the self-hypnotic exercise and get on with your endeavors, a giant step closer to your goal of achieving fluid, free-flowing speech.

As for other nervous habits, humans have a host of little ways of fussing with themselves that at the very least present a negative picture and at the worst are self-damaging. An individual may bite his nails, pick his nose or ears, crack his knuckles, drum his fingers, play with his hair or engage in fidgety movements so apparently involuntary that they appear to be tics. We look peculiar when we do such things, and people understandably come to negative conclusions about us.

The habitual nail biter, let us say, is harming himself in the eyes of others in two ways: people watch and feel a little repelled, and they also sense that such a person has lost control. If he can't control himself in that area, they conclude, somewhat below the level of consciousness perhaps, then he can't control himself in other areas, either.

But whether people see him or not, the critical point is that to the extent that he has to keep biting his nails such a person is not in charge of himself; he feels so compelled to follow such practices that the choice has been taken out of living. He needs to do something to reestablish mastery over his own actions. If he chooses self-hypnosis as the means, both aspects of the offending habit—its effect on him and also what others think about it—should be woven into the syllogism:

"For my feeling of being in charge of my life, as well as for the respect of others, chewing on my nails [or whatever the annoying habit may be] is a harmful act.

"I need to be in charge of my life and to have others' respect to live contentedly.

"To the degree I want to live contentedly, I will be the guardian of my nails."

In the visualizing that follows, he may wish to engage in a bit of substitution. That is, with eyes still closed he would see himself, on that imaginary screen on the wall, beginning to bring his hand to his mouth to bite his nails. But instead, the hand bypasses the mouth and glides up to his forehead to brush back a strand of hair, then falls to his side, where it rests calmly and comfortably. Or the hands may be employed in some constructive action such as picking up a pad and pencil to make notes on tomorrow's plans.

In addition to the substitutive approach, the individual may wish to imagine himself holding his hands up and looking at his fingernails, picturing them at the length that is most desirable. As you look at the screen and see yourself inspecting your nails, a smile of satisfaction comes over your face, brought there by the knowledge that your nails are of a size and shape pleasing to you and to any onlooker. Finally, imagine that another person enters the scene, gazes at your nails admiringly and comments on how good they look.

The person with a different but related nervous habit would take a similar tack in his imagery by devising some action as a substitute for the unwanted habit. As the hand is about to perform the offending action, let it land somewhere else. For instance, if a man, you may bring your hand to your cheek to see whether you need a shave; if a woman, you might reach in your purse to check on some object there.

Then follows the positive picture, seeing oneself on the screen, with hands in lap, on the knees, at one's sides or occupied in some harmless fashion, perhaps with pencil and paper. The individual imagining such a scene feels in concert with himself and with the universe and, smiling down at his hands, thinks: "These are my hands, and they're controlled by my head. I'm in charge of them and can place them wherever I want them, and they'll feel quite comfortable. I'm at my ease. I feel gratified and revel in being master of my fingers, my hands and my entire body. *I* am in control."

And after emerging from the exercise, it's enormously satisfying to know that just as you were in control during your self-hypnotic exercise, you can continue to be in control in your normal everyday state of consciousness.

CHAPTER 7

How To Master Emotional Problems

B y way of introduction to this chapter, I would like to tell you about a man who came to me for help in controlling his anger. This man, president of a small but successful corporation, would find himself engaging in angry outbursts at his employees, with very little provocation. The consequences of his fury were twofold: sometimes he would get so enraged that he fired the employee, and other times the employee would become so distressed that he quit. Naturally, this man's company had a steady turnover of personnel.

When he first visited me, I informed him that digging to the roots of his anger might take some time and that my recommendation was that we do this through psychoanalysis. Because of the immediacy of his problem, however, I proposed a shortcut method at the outset before he lost his company altogether.

So, after preliminary history taking, I suggested that he close his eyes and imagine that in front of him was the usual white movie screen. He was to project a three-dimensional image of himself on that screen and tell me what he saw.

In a few moments he answered, "I see myself there. I'm short and plump, fat-cheeked. My fists are clenched, and my face is contorted in distress and anger."

I next asked him to talk to that figure, to "tell that image of 'you' up there on the screen just what you'd like of him."

Eventually he murmured, "I want you to be tall, six inches taller than I am. Slim. Strong. Calm. I'm an evangelist, and there's a vast audience in front of me. I hold them in my palm. I no longer have to be angry, because I am perfect and I am leading other people to perfection."

"Now if you will pause for a moment," I interjected, "and examine that person you've just described on the screen, do you have any comment?"

With his eyes still closed, he chuckled and said, "How can I be that tall? I can get thinner, but can I grow six inches at my age? An evangelist? Out of the question. What's going on in me?"

"Could it be," I answered, "that you have an ideal of perfection for yourself that's unattainable, and that you're constantly looking at the broad canyon that separates what you are from what you think you should be?"

I told him I was reminded of a passage in John F. Kennedy's *Profiles in Courage* that I frequently quote to my patients. It concerns John Quincy Adams at the peak of his career. A brilliant man who had been an eloquent member of Congress, minister to several European courts as well as ambassador to the Court of St. James's, Adams had come up from Secretary of State to be the President of the United States. As Kennedy wrote of him, the second President Adams had held more important offices and participated in more momentous events than anyone else in the history of our nation. While President of the United States, this tower of a man wrote in his diary, "I can scarcely recollect a single instance of success in anything that I ever undertook."

So I said to my patient, "If John Quincy Adams could see himself as a complete failure, when in the eyes of the nation he was the greatest of men, perhaps you have the right to have a little problem of that sort. Just what is that problem? Technically, it's a discrepancy between ego and ego ideal. More simply, there's a gap between the successful person you are and the perfect person no one can be. Just as Adams's conscience must have been tormenting him—'Sure, you're President of the United States, but are you President of the planet?'—yours must be nagging you—'President of a fine corporation, but are you President of General Motors?'

"Maybe the anger you're lavishing on members of your company comes from your own frustration at not being the perfect president of a dream corporation, and it has nothing to do with these people or your actual shortcomings, but rather with an ideal that you've set too high for yourself."

Before he left I showed him how to induce the hypnotic state and suggested that in that state he talk to himself along the lines we'd discussed.

The man came back in a couple of weeks—he had been out of town on a business trip—and reported that he had been sampling this method of bringing about a relaxed state on his own and trying to establish his ideal at a more realistic level. In doing so he kept reminding himself that it was all right to be president of a successful organization, and if he kept his eye on this reality rather than on a point out beyond a never-never horizon, he could remain calm.

He commented that he felt he had a long way to go to pull in his ego ideal, but that while working on it he found his outbursts of anger lessening in number and intensity. Progress continued in succeeding weeks as he and his corporation, to say nothing of a more stable labor force, prospered.

We should emphasize here, lest the moral of this story be misconstrued, that we are in no way suggesting that you should not be ambitious and set goals for yourself. The point is that the goals can be realistic, attainable ones and that you can enjoy and be proud of your achievements rather than forever lamenting your limitations. If your nature is such that your reach always exceeds your grasp, how can you help but be frustrated and disappointed? You may strive for improvement, but along the way you might allow yourself some pride and pleasure in the things you do accomplish.

In the case of the angry businessman, not only was his ego ideal so inflated that no one short of Zeus could live up to it, but the frustration and uncontrollable anger generated as he sought perfection were making life miserable both for himself and those around him.

The intent of this chapter is to help you gain mastery over your emotions, whether they be excessive or insufficient, so that your emotional response is appropriate for you under the circumstances. For example, it's certainly justifiable to be depressed on occasion. The death of a friend or relative, a serious illness, a great disappointment are all causes for sadness rather than joy. It's when sorrow becomes excessive or chronic, *e.g.,* when you go into mourning for years over the death of an uncle, that the emotional response becomes suspect.

The lack of emotion can likewise be questioned. If, for instance, someone abuses you verbally at a social gathering or throws a drink in your face, and you merely smile wanly and silently walk away, later you might reflect, "I should have been mad about that; why wasn't I?" In such a case some degree of anger would appear to be justifiable and its absence inappropriate.

Just as periodic sadness and occasional anger may be legitimate, so may fear. Anyone who remains fearless in close proximity to a runaway lion would be a fool, though probably not for long. Realistic fear may be essential to self-preservation, while prolonged or irrational fear is quite a different matter. The latter condition is seen in the recluse who retreats into a shuttered and cluttered house, isolated from the threats of the outside world.

In short, there is an appropriate time for grief, for anger, for fear—for any emotion. But not *all* of the time or, on the other hand, *none* of the time. Emotions are suitable some of the time, under certain circumstances: that is, in the time and place and situation which is appropriate for *you.*

We're not advocating democratization of emotion here, that everyone should respond the same way given the same stimuli. An appropriate response is one *usually* shared by others, but not necessarily so. An appropriate response for everyone if a theater catches fire is to get out. But, to continue the theater analogy, an appropriate response for *nearly* everyone in a Paris theater in 1913, on first hearing the discordant score of Stravinsky's radical *Rite of Spring,* was the same: anger and flight. But if you had been in that theater and had found the music brilliant and exciting, the appropriate response for you under the circumstances would have been to stay and cheer as others fled and jeered.

So the fact that your emotional responses may not be those of the majority does not invalidate them. It should, however, call for some introspection on your part. If your reaction holds up after examination, fine: it's right for you. But when your response, regardless of how others react, doesn't feel right to you, that's cause for some action. If it makes you uncomfortable, anxious, sad, angry or whatever, then the emotional response may very well be inappropriate for you and you may want to do something about it.

Let me point out, however, that we're not trying to stop people from expressing themselves. On the contrary, therapists of all sorts, whether they be hypnotherapists, behavioral therapists, psychoanalysts, etc., devote much of their time to helping people express emotions more freely. We're not out to repress or even suppress. What we hope to do is to peel off any excess emotion—fear or anger or sadness or anxiety—and leave a core of freely expressed feelings that work to one's advantage.

The question arises, how do you know whether your emotions are excessive? There are several criteria to help you judge. First, your own estimate: "I just feel it was overdone; I overreacted." You yourself sense that something is awry.

Second, the response of your friends and other people around you. If you find that they're looking at you strangely or turning away, you have a clue that your emotions may be excessive.

Third, not just people but things get out of whack: you trip over your own feet, knock over a glass, spill your coffee, etc.

If you don't feel you're "losing your marbles," if people are well-disposed toward you and if everything stays in place, your emotion is probably well placed.

On the other hand, your emotional response may be insufficient. How do you know whether that's the case? You use the same criteria as for excessive emotional display: self, other people and things. The therapist may say to his patient, "Did you get angry when he said that to you? You didn't? It seems to me anger would have been appropriate; don't you think so?"

"Now that you mention it," the patient might respond, "when he said my mother was an alcoholic just because she takes a drink every six months, and he said it publicly so that it was printed in the newspaper the next day, sure, I guess I *should* have been angry." On reflection, he sees his emotional reaction as wanting.

Another example. If shots ring out in the night outside one's house and, as shouting fills the air, one continues to read poetry in his easy chair, a neighbor might observe, "That person is not showing appropriate concern for what's happening around him."

Or if you're at a football game and everyone is on his feet jumping around, waving flags and yelling, while you just sit there feeling rather sad, the conduct of the other people there might tip you off that there's something inappropriate about yours at the time.

Finally, the third criterion, "Do I suppress my feelings when external events would seem to warrant having some?" For example, if the house is burning down around you and you don't have any feelings about it, you may perish.

Feeling is such a rich, vibrant part of living when experienced in a comfortable and productive way. That will be the aim of this chapter: mastering your emotional problems in order to feel most in tune with yourself and the world.

Fears and Phobias

"The only thing we have to fear," declared President Franklin Delano Roosevelt in the depths of the Depression, "is fear itself."

He recognized the paralyzing potential of fear and rallied a dispirited people into banishing it from the national psyche. Morbid fear, as distinct from the constructive kind of fear that keeps us away from a rattlesnake or a blazing building, can be just as crippling for an individual as for a nation.

One may have a fear of events (an upcoming speech, for example), people (or animals), or things (such as elevators or airplanes). I'll not attempt in this chapter to cover every conceivable fear a person could harbor, but will discuss common ones from each of the aforementioned categories. These will serve as paradigms, then, for applying this method of self-hypnosis to conquer any other fears the reader may dream up. ("Dream up" is an apt term, I feel, for we do tend to concoct fears.)

To begin, let us say there is a public-speaking situation approaching. It may be an appearance before television cameras, on a platform, in front of townspeople, before the board of directors, with the sewing circle, for the school class, etc. Stage fright is a frequent complaint even among those who make their living appearing before the public. Marilyn Monroe, for example, used hypnosis to overcome her stage fright, and in my own practice I treat actors not only for their fear of performing but also for "freezing" at auditions.

To overcome stage fright, several times a day for several days before the event, the individual is advised to practice the customary relaxation exercise, then to induce the state of self-hypnosis and mentally recite a syllogism along these lines:

"For my feelings of self-worth, fear and trembling as I appear before this audience is ruinous.

"I need my feelings of self-worth to live in any kind of comfort.

"To the degree that I wish to live comfortably, I will protect my feelings of self-worth as I would protect [name of loved one]."

Such a syllogism can be used in a variety of situations, whether a public-speaking event or an encounter with a figure of authority, such as the boss or some eminent stranger. For instance, the young musician who is to be introduced to a luminary in his field may shiver with fright, but he can prepare himself ahead of time with a syllogism, using wording fitting to him:

"For my feelings of self-value, to shiver and shake in the presence of Leonard Bernstein is poisonous.

"I need my feelings of self-value in order to function effectively.

"To the degree that I want to function effectively, I will feel quite at ease as I look Mr. Bernstein straight in the eye, with my blood pressure and pulse normal, and my voice steady."

Following the syllogism comes the visualization: as you approach the feared person or event, you see yourself feeling on top of the world, with a smile on your face. "This is where I belong," you say to yourself. We've all thought of some person we've seen perform or speak before an audience, "He's obviously 'at home'; it's as if he belonged there." Now you see yourself on that imaginary screen, "at home" and radiating pleasure, externally visible and internally felt. You feel strong, able, relaxed and in full charge of yourself and your emotions.

Follow this visualization with a posthypnotic suggestion: "I will find that I'll feel right 'at home' there, just as if I were talking to my family and dearest friends. I'll feel vibrant, abundant enthusiasm as I approach [boss, famous person, principal, whomever] and be so caught up in my purpose and eager to communicate that my mood will be contagious and will be received agreeably, positively. It will all be easy. When I emerge from this relaxed state I will feel confident that everything will work out to my advantage." Whereupon you terminate the self-hypnotic exercise in the usual way.

Let us turn then from this rather broad-based, generalized fear to the more specific fears called phobias. These, as we may know, range from agoraphobia (fear of open places) to zoophobia (fear of animals). They may be fairly common, such as fear of flying, or esoteric: for example, lyssophobia (fear of dissolving).

In this chapter we will deal with some popular fears and let these examples serve as prototypes for treatment of your own disturbing phobias. In the syllogism, you will simply substitute "fear of———" (whatever's troubling you) for the phobia described here, and then create the appropriate imagery in the subsequent stage of self-hypnosis.

Let's consider fear of flying first. You're at home the night before the scheduled flight. Select for yourself a quiet, comfortable spot, make yourself relaxed and induce the state of self-hypnosis. Next, mentally recite the syllogism, using such wording as:

"For my feelings of self-esteem, the fear of flying is ruinous.

"I need my feelings of self-esteem to function ably.

"To the degree that I wish to function ably, I will protect my feelings of self-esteem as I would protect [name of a loved one]."

Then the imagery. The key concept to your visualizing is to join yourself to the plane. The airplane fear, I submit, is based on fighting the plane, on making you and the flying machine adversaries rather than partners. Instead of fighting the plane, I, the person about to fly, want to make myself part of the aircraft, just like a wing, one of the instruments or one of the seats. I picture myself first, on the imaginary movie screen in my mind's eye, en route to the airport. I sit in the car or bus happily whistling, looking forward to the flight with pleasure. I experience a kind of light and airy feeling, almost like floating.

Now I arrive at the airport, and I'm in the terminal waiting for the flight. I'm feeling very relaxed, quite content, in a state resembling floating. I'm on my way from the terminal to the airplane itself. I don't care whether the sun is shining or it's cloudy; the plane looks beautiful to me, and I'm looking forward to the flight, feeling quite light and comfortable.

I'm seated in the plane now, and I'm part of it. The seat is bolted to the floor of the airplane, and I'm part of that seat. We are as one. I feel that this is where I belong. Again, there's that feeling of being "at home." I'm part of the airplane, and I'm going to float with it—free, light, airy, easy, smiling, happy.

As the plane moves down the runway and glides into the sky, just as all the parts of it move as a unit, I am unified with it. I see the plane take off, and I see myself, smiling and enthusiastic, as part of the plane, floating. This is home. Every minute is a pleasure as I occupy myself gazing at the clouds rolling by, chatting, dozing, watching a movie.

Similarly, as the plane is about to land, a time when some people worry about crashing, I screen out any such negative thoughts by picturing the plane exactly right in its approach. The pilot is well trained and experienced and knows his business. The plane is in his charge, and I am part of the plane. As we approach the ground we are in perfect control. The plane—and I—land smoothly and easily. Before emerging from self-hypnosis, I may then plant the posthypnotic suggestion that just as I have pictured my coming flight in my imagination, so shall it occur in reality.

You may indulge in the exercise during the days before the flight, at home on the day of the flight, en route to the airport, at the airport waiting for the departure of the airplane, on the plane awaiting takeoff, during the flight and while landing— any of these times or all of them.

Not so different from the fear of flying is fear of high places: disaster is expected when high up. The person in an airplane is afraid the plane will go out of control, while the person in a high place, looking out of a window or over a ledge, gets a sickening feeling as if he were falling; indeed, he fears that he *will* either fall or jump.

During his self-hypnosis, the person afraid of heights will substitute "fear of heights" for "fear of flying" in the syllogism. In his imagery, he may picture himself on a roof, let us say, looking down over a ledge. He sees himself as part of that ledge and therefore feels safe and comfortable, because he knows the ledge isn't going to fall. The ledge is part of the roof, the roof is part of the building, and the building is firmly fixed in the solid ground. It's this kind of succession of "nailing down" that will have one feeling safe and secure.

The person uneasy with heights will see himself now as being in a state of comfort, with a smile on his face and with his heartbeat steady. He has the feeling that his feet are rooted, locked, nailed into whatever flooring he's standing on, and his hands are steady and sure on the ledge he's leaning on. Just as there is a feeling of being in concert with the airplane while flying, there's the feeling of being in harmony with the roof ledge or window sill.

Let's consider the opposite extreme: fear of closed places (claustrophobia). The claustrophobic person fears that one of two things will happen: either the ceiling, walls and floor of the small space he's in are going to close in and crush him, or his source of air will be cut off and he'll be smothered. We'll assume that neither could realistically happen.

Now, this situation is just the opposite of that of the person who fears heights. In the latter case, the person imagines himself as part of the moving object or part of the building, whereas the claustrophobic person needs to see himself as *distinct* from the feared closed space. In his imagery, he will picture himself as a separate entity. The walls are firmly fixed apart from him, the ceiling will stay where it is, and the air will continue to flow into the room as he enjoys a feeling of floating comfort.

"When I emerge from this state," he may tell himself, "I will find that upon entry into that eight-by-eight-foot room, I won't care how small the space; I will be in perfect comfort. The walls and ceiling will stay at more than arm's length, the airflow will be continuous and certain, and I will be smiling and at my ease, enjoying my new-found mastery of the situation."

Let's consider now another favorite phobia, the fear of animals: dogs, cats, snakes, mice, bats, spiders, ferrets or any other creature furred, feathered or finned.

As with so many emotional disruptions, phobias quite often have their roots in childhood, even infant, experiences. I myself can attest to this fact, for I had a dog phobia I trace back to a kindergarten experience.

I remember bounding along the street on my way home from kindergarten one day, when a dog started bounding along beside me. The more I ran, the more he ran, and the more both of us ran, the more frightened I became. Apparently I transmitted the message to this animal, because he reached up for my swinging hand as I ran along in fright, and bit it. That was the end of dogs for me for a number of years, not an atypical beginning to a phobia. (Incidentally, my story bears out the curious James-Lange theory of emotion. Harvard scientists James Lange and William James theorized in the late 1800s that we are afraid of the dog *because* we run from him, not the reverse.)

To apply self-hypnosis to conquering the dog phobia, one would induce the hypnotic state, then recite a syllogism:

"For my feelings of self-mastery, fear of dogs is poisonous.

"I need my feelings of self-mastery to live comfortably.

"To the degree I want to live comfortably, I'll feel in a state of ease in the presence of dogs."

Following the syllogism, the individual who fears dogs sees a series of scenes played out in the theater of his imagination. Suppose, like mine, his fear dates back to a childhood experience. Let him first picture himself as a child standing outside a fenced yard. On the other side of the fence he sees a dog running about. The child is very happy he's outside the fence.

Step two in this little drama is to observe someone, perhaps his father, lean over the fence and hold out his hand. The dog sidles up, sniffs the hand and bounds away. Moments pass, then the dog comes back to the fence and licks the father's hand. In step three, the dog allows the man to pet him. The boy observes all this in a state of delight and wonder; he's quite safe with the fence between him and that gigantic beast.

Then the boy, identifying with his father, wants to do the same thing he did, and so he pokes his finger gingerly through the fence. The dog sniffs, licks and nuzzles the boy's hand. Father may then go into the yard and frolic with the dog, which jumps about and rolls happily on the grass. And finally, in the culmination of this behavioristic exercise to lessen the fear of animals, the boy himself enters the yard and plays with the friendly, loving dog.

One point to remember: it's quite possible that you frighten the dog as much as he frightens you. The concept of mastery is carried beyond your getting over your fear of the dog to the point that *you* help the dog be unafraid of you. The comforting of another seems to put one in a state of mastery, *e.g.,* a patient of mine who eased his own fear of flying by reassuring the passenger sitting next to him.

See yourself in the role of the comforter: "Now look, doggie, you don't have to be afraid of me. That's it, just calm down. I like you; you're my friend." Strangely enough, this *will* quiet the dog's feelings, and these friendly vibrations will bounce back and forth from dog to person, and both will feel better.

Finally, before terminating the exercise you may give yourself a posthypnotic suggestion such as: "After I emerge from this state and see my first dog, the thought will come to me, 'How can I help that dog be nice and calm so that he won't be frightened of me?'"

Sadness or Depression

By and large, there are three general categories of sadness:

(1) Chronic sadness. A dull state, very dependable and very miserable. Chronic sadness is either constant or it has some periodicity to it—every morning, every Sunday, every menstrual period, whenever one sees a seriously ill friend or relative.

(2) Acute sadness. Much sharper, such sadness has no cycle, no regularity to it. Rather it is a reaction to a specific event, such as a business reversal or a frustrated romance.

(3) Depression. We usually consider true depression as lying outside the neurotic spectrum and in the area of psychosis. It may constitute the "down" phase of the manic-depressive cycle, or it may characterize the person who just goes down and stays there, possibly to be institutionalized. We will not attempt to deal with the third category, the psychotic depressive, in this book.

Instead, we will concern ourselves with the neurotic person who chooses to defend his chronic sadness as a kind of low mood enveloping many if not most of the events of his life. If he gets up late, he's sad; if he gets up early, that makes him sad. If his wife is grouchy, he sulks; if she's cheerful, *he* grumps around. His sadness is not incapacitating, as it is with the psychotic, but it impinges upon his ability to function—and it's a damn nuisance. Such a person may decide, "I'd like to get rid of my negative feelings and feel better."

After induction of the state of high relaxation and focused concentration comes the syllogism:

"For my feelings of self-mastery and well-being, this prevailing 'down' mood of mine is poisonous.

"I need my sense of self-mastery and well-being in order to exist comfortably.

"To the degree that I want to live comfortably, I will stand guard over my feelings of well-being, protecting them as I would protect my treasured [name of loved one]."

Then we move into the customary visualization. If the individual is a woman, she imagines a picture of herself on the fantasy movie screen in front of her. There she is, her head bowed, her shoulders slumped, wrapped in a shroud of gloom. Then she watches herself throw her shoulders back, pull her head up, open her droopy eyes wide and let a good feeling flow through her veins and course throughout her whole body and up into her head, where it elicits a bright, broad smile.

And she sees herself there on the screen feeling sunny, alive, buoyant, even joyful. Her spirits are obviously quite high, not outside a realistic range but just comfortably high, as she moves through the various activities of her life.

Perhaps she sees her husband's expression of surprise as he remarks, "My, you're cheerful today!" and she replies, "Well, that's just the way I feel." If it's not her husband, it's a good friend commenting on her jaunty mood. Or her cat.

Then she sees herself walking down the street. Her step is light and springy. She looks at the people, buildings and trees with renewed interest. She sees life around her as new and fresh today. She watches herself in cheerful association with others at her work or, if she works alone, she whistles as she tends to her occupation.

Finally, she suggests to herself in her self-induced relaxation that she has the ability in reality to feel like the person on the screen. Then she brings herself out of the relaxed state.

Turning from chronic, generalized sadness, let's consider

the acute variety as exemplified by Mr. Om. A native of a Southeast Asian country, Mr. Om came to me in a state of extreme sadness. He explained that normally he was a light-hearted individual who took life more cheerfully than most people, so that he was somewhat surprised to find himself in his present dismal frame of mind. The cause, however, was no mystery. The stock market had dropped sharply, and Mr. Om, who had been dealing in puts and calls, suddenly found himself $35,000 in debt.

His plight had him waking in the morning feeling miserable, not wanting to get out of bed, not wanting to eat—and once at the office not even wanting to find out the state of the stock market, and if he did, almost not caring. This attitude of complete surrender, utterly foreign to him, had brought him to me.

Since Mr. Om was simply passing through New York, he had neither the time nor the resources to engage in long-term analysis. I used our one session together to teach him self-hypnosis.

Because I wanted to avoid getting bogged down in a language problem, I did not present a verbal syllogism to this man from a foreign country. Instead, we went right to the visualization of the white screen on the wall.

I suggested to him that he see himself, on that imaginary screen, walking down the street, as he would when he left my office, in a state of ease. Rather than being all bottled up within himself, he would look about and take notice of the sky and the buildings and the people around him. He would see himself as feeling tall and strong and able. He would be aware that the stock market goes up and down and that he has no control over its fluctuations. Further, he would recognize that world forces and he are two different beings, that the stock market and he were quite separate entities, that money and he were separate and distinct.

We now had him looking at himself feeling quite strong and able and in charge of himself. We had him returning home in his imagination, being greeted by his concerned wife and reassuring her that all was going to be well, that whatever happened they still had their love for each other and they had their family, which was a thing beyond price. There was nothing to fear, nothing to worry about; things were in his control.

Then I had him visualize calling his broker, getting some news and feeling quite comfortable about it. "I see, that's the situation," he might say. "Therefore, let's take this action." Then he would put down the phone and return to work with zest and concentration, in a state of ease.

Finally, there was the posthypnotic suggestion that before he ended his hypnosis he would tell himself, "I'm about to emerge from this state. When I do, I will find myself quite in control of my usual sensations, feelings and muscular responses, and I will now be quite calm. The world will look bright and promising to me. I will feel in harmony with the world and with the future. Come what may, I will meet it ably."

As he left my office, Mr. Om said he felt quite comfortable and relaxed, and asked how much my bill would be. "You can't afford anything: go," I told him. And he did.

Some three weeks later I received a long-distance call from Mr. Om. Obviously in good spirits, he informed me that he had been practicing self-hypnosis faithfully, that it was working and, although he was still heavily in debt, his work was going well and he now saw his way out of his financial crisis.

You may fairly observe that anyone faced with Mr. Om's money problems, or with any such dilemma, has a right to feel sad. I agree. Indulge your misery for a while if that will make you feel better (we'd best not open up *that* Pandora's box here, the pleasure of pain), but to be in extended "mourning for my life," as a Chekhov character explains her mood, hobbles your ability to rectify a negative situation. Unless Mr. Om, after a suitably short period of mourning for *his* life, changed his mental bent and began to function productively at work, he might very well manage to lose his means of livelihood and sink deeper and deeper into debt and depression.

If your sad state of mind interferes with your earning a living, colors your relationships with others and/or has you feeling a way you prefer not to feel, I suggest you engage in the kind of mood-elevating imagery prescribed for Mr. Om.

Anger (Hostility), Irritability, Hate

It's fitting that we take up anger and its variations just after sadness or depression, for we observe that people flop from one to the other quite easily. One is often a defense against the other. If we get underneath the anger and relieve the person of that defense, he may fall into depression. On the other hand, pull a person out of his chronic low mood, and he often starts getting angry with people around him. The two frequently operate in that fashion. However, the fact that one may replace the other is no excuse for clinging to either one; both are negative emotions and both deserve correcting.

Whether it precedes sadness or follows it, anger interferes with easy, comfortable living. We should emphasize at the outset that the anger we're talking about here is not the brief, justifiable outburst all of us engage in on occasion and which may advisedly be freely expressed and expended, rather than allowed to smoulder inside. What we're dealing with now is the frequent or intense variety that either gets us into trouble with others ("What in hell is wrong with him?" someone might say about an eruption of anger) or, turned inward ("I'm mad at myself"), can be very self-hurtful.

Along with anger we often find hate, hostility and aggression, either physical or nonphysical, or at the other extreme, impatience and annoyance. Although there are shades of difference among them, therapeutically we approach them in the same manner, using the self-hypnotic exercise to tackle whatever phase of the emotion is causing trouble.

Anger, as with other negative emotions, can be contagious—to the detriment of your physical condition if you happen to be five-two and get mad at a strapping six-footer. Anger can also be transmitted from one person to another, even when the second party is the proverbial innocent bystander. I observe that when a patient in my consulting room gets angry in my presence, not necessarily at *me*, I pick up some of the same emotion. For example, a woman was recently describing to me her anger toward her mother, who lived with her and made great demands upon her. As my patient reexperienced her anger in my presence, I could feel the muscles in my own hands, stomach and shoulders tighten, as if ready to begin a flow of adrenalin and make me angry if I let it continue.

Anger can also be literally and physically self-damaging. I'm reminded of a clinical experiment in which perspiration was taken from the body of an angry man and placed on the tongue of a laboratory rat, whereupon the animal showed every sign of having been poisoned. So the use of the word "poison" in the syllogism is particularly apt in the case of anger:

"For my body, not for me but for my body, anger is a poison.

"I need my body to live.

"To the degree I want to live, I will preserve my body as I would preserve a loved member of my family."

If your troubling brand of anger happens to be overt aggression that has you doing all you can to restrain yourself from hauling off and splitting the other guy's lip, and in some cases actually taking the action, you're concerned not just with your own body but, more immediately, with your relationships with others. If this is your problem, you may wish to alter the syllogism to something such as:

"For my relationships with others, not for me but for my comfortable relationships with people, my aggression is poisonous.

"I need my agreeable relationships with other people in order to exist.

"To the degree I want to exist, I will give my relationships with other people the same loving protection I give ————."

Let me encourage you to engage in imagery after this verbal implant: keeping your eyes closed, in that relaxed state of mind where concentration is at its peak, see yourself on the make-believe movie screen in front of you.

Allow only positive pictures to appear on that screen, only positive feelings to flow through the body you're looking at. Picture that person as one who is in a loving state of mind, flooded with feelings of good will, principally toward you. "I feel well toward myself," let that figure on the wall say, while at the same time experiencing a quiet, easy, caring acceptance of self.

Next, see the figure on the screen send those feelings out to someone important in his life: mother, father, son, daughter, wife or husband, best friend. Watch these warm feelings flood your body and radiate out toward the other person: tender, giving, affectionate vibrations toward the other person, who responds with similar sympathetic feelings.

Then change the scene and switch those positive feelings toward someone who has the ability to irritate you. Picture yourself with that person, letting his or her barbs go sailing harmlessly by as you continue to send out signals of sympathy, gentle acceptance, regard, even love for the other person.

This may be followed by a posthypnotic suggestion to the effect that whenever an impulse toward unwanted anger may arise, the image of the person on the screen—calm, sympathetic, forgiving—will pop into mind.

Shyness (Timidity)

These two, shyness and timidity, mean essentially the same thing—a kind of modified fear, fear of other people and fear of situations. The timidity is a sign of low self-esteem and a cause of lowered esteem from others.

While it's to a person's advantage to hold his tongue and his peace in many instances, his reticence should spring rather from a sense of well-being than from a fear of exposing or committing himself. It's not the quietness itself we're trying to get at here, but the state of mind that lies behind the external behavior. We want to modify the shy person's perceptions of himself and of the outer world so that he may feel comfortable in situations in which it has formerly been his custom to feel timid. On occasion he may then choose to remain silent, but it will be *his* choice; he will feel just as comfortable if he asserts himself and speaks out. He should be the master of his responses, not the reverse.

The individual who would learn to shed his timidity may begin in the usual fashion, by first inducing the state of self-hypnosis and then mentally stating a syllogism, the wording of which may go something like this:

"For my own growth, timidity is a restricting poison.

"I need growth in order to make my life worthwhile.

"To the degree that I want my life to be worthwhile, I will further my own growth as I would further the growth of my beloved ———."

For the imagery, the timid person envisions himself standing tall, walking straight, firm of foot and face and gesture. He pictures himself smiling, moving confidently into a group and calmly but positively asserting himself; the people in that group are eager to hear him and are interested in what he might have to say.

This is the person whose manner and conduct heretofore had conveyed an apology for living, the timid soul afraid of his own shadow. Let him now imagine asserting himself—easily, freely, comfortably, boldly but without force—in any situation in which he tends to feel shy. If it has been his practice to be frightened of his boss, let him imagine meeting with the boss.

It's time for the appointment. He opens the office door with a feeling of calm and ease, walks in, approaches his boss and shakes his hand, smiling and relaxed, in charge of himself and the situation. He sees his boss congratulating him: "You certainly are coming along well in your work here and in your whole manner. You appear to be changing. It seems you're becoming more your own man. Keep it up." He thanks the boss and feels on a par with him as he walks out, smiling and head held high.

Where do you become shy or timid? Are you reluctant to tell the clerk who's trying to sell you a suit of clothes that it isn't for you and that he should find you what you do want? Picture yourself standing your ground on the screen. You say to him, "This is not quite what I had in mind; get me a brown one." Or, "I see it's getting late. I'm going to have to leave now; we haven't found quite what I want. Goodby."

In whatever situation you find yourself constricted, envision yourself as possessed of that kind of freedom that allows you to assert yourself positively to make things happen in your favor. See yourself as meeting the world in a free and comfortable self-affirming fashion.

Following the visualization and before emerging from the raised state, you may give yourself a posthypnotic suggestion incorporating such thoughts as: "I will come to feel freer and more comfortable with each passing day. My thinking will be increasingly positive. Each day I will find myself feeling more in charge of myself, more self-possessed, more self-assertive. If things don't always go perfectly, my faith in myself will remain strong. I will feel the freedom to concentrate, to remember, to think clearly. Increasingly, I will experience a sense of being at peace with myself, relaxed. My feeling will be one of moving forward, of taking positive steps to improve my state of being and my state of mind."

Such a sampling—the reader's imagination undoubtedly will produce more—suggests the type of verbal implants designed to replace timid thoughts with positive ones.

Nervousness, Anxiety, Tension

Along with nervousness, we will include in this discussion two very near relatives, worry and anxiety, and two distant cousins, apprehension and tension. We're not attempting to categorize these in a scholarly way. Rather, we're saying that an exploration of nervousness gives us an opportunity to talk about related conditions.

In addition to being emotionally draining, all of these negative feelings can erupt into such physical symptoms as headache, stomach upset, quickened pulse, etc. I am convinced that these emotions have bodily consequences the extent of which has not yet been grasped. There is even speculation that the formation of malignant cells that multiply so rapidly and fatally in cancer might be a function of negative emotions. There are scientists who, at least privately if not publicly, will say that the patient who is helped out of a negative state of mind is a better bet for cure of cancer.

Twenty years ago it would have taken quite an imagination for someone to say, in effect, "For my *body* I will stop smoking." More likely he would have said, "Smoking hurts my body? What're you talking about? The smoke goes through my nostrils, and it feels, smells and tastes fine! What does that have to do with cancer and emphysema and heart trouble?"

Today, however, even the Surgeon General has determined that "Cigarette Smoking Is Dangerous to Your Health." But would he declare that "Nervousness Is . . ."? I do. And I propose that you let yourself halt this killer. The person who is feeling upset and nervous begins with a syllogism:

"For my health—physical and emotional—not for me but for my health, nervousness [anxiety, tension, whatever it may be] is a poison.

"I need my physical and emotional health to live in contentment.

"To the degree that I want to live in contentment, I'll allow myself to feel calm and peaceful."

Having induced self-hypnosis and recited a syllogism, now imagine yourself on the wall screen. See yourself in that favorite geographical spot that helps you bring about this relaxed state. Perhaps you're at a beach—my own favorite is on a Caribbean island. There I am, stretched out on the warm sand. It's a calm, restful scene. I am awake, but my muscles are flaccid. I may deliberately raise each limb and let it drop back in order to induce a further relaxed state. I let the sun beam down on my face and on my body, and I am devoid of any muscle movement.

Then, some noise starts up alongside me. I am aware, as I lie there on the beach, that people around me are having their fun. It's loud, and I can tell there's a lot of movement, even though my eyes are closed. I hear shouts and laughter and loud talking, but as a patient of mine once expressed it, "I turn down the volume." As I turn down the volume of the noise— or at least my perception of the noise—I seem quite unaffected by the hubbub around me, and I just continue to lie there, basking in the warm sunshine and the soft sea breezes.

There is a double purpose in such imagery: to gain the ability to be calm oneself when the scene is calm, and in moments of stress, when people around us are excited or disturbed, to likewise remain calm.

As you continue to watch yourself on the screen—lying on the beach, fishing in a rowboat, reclining in bed, sunning yourself on a roof or in whatever calm situation you conjure up—you may pronounce some positive suggestions to yourself. Some samples:

"There I am, fully self-possessed. That's the state that I am increasingly experiencing. Each day I will feel this self-possession enlarging. More and more I will think and talk about pleasant subjects. [We refrain from saying, 'I will not think about morbid things.' This brings up the morbidity, and it's difficult to avoid thinking of a subject once you tell yourself not to think of it, like trying not to think of a purple elephant.]

"I will deliberately direct my thinking toward pleasing matters. I will notice that my confidence and my feeling of self-conquest are on the rise. I will find it easier and easier to relax. I will increasingly develop mental poise and peace of mind. As others rush about, I will find myself becoming more and more tranquil and serene. My ability to control my emotional life will grow day by day."

Now, what are the life situations that tend to bring on attacks of nervousness or anxiety? Keeping an important appointment or making an urgent telephone call are examples. As the dreaded hour approaches, a person may find himself getting increasingly nervous. What to do? I like the approach Dr. Herbert Benson takes in his book, *The Relaxation Response*. He says that the aim should not be simply to remain calm in the face of a usually upsetting external event, but actually to reverse the process: as the disturbing event gets closer and closer, one gets more and more calm. In other words, each moment as a difficult situation approaches—the speech I have to give, that meeting with my superior, a big date—the quieter

I become, the more at ease I feel, the more subdued I find my feelings to be.

One may so picture the situation. Let us say you're in the anteroom of the famous person you have an appointment with and you notice that people around you are nervous and fidgety. You, on the other hand, sit there in a state of smiling calm, with muscles quite relaxed. In your movie screen imagery, let the people around you be concerned and worried; you stand apart, calm, cool, confident.

Let's consider another situation involving anxiety: a mother worried about her fourteen-year-old daughter traveling through the snow some dark night to accomplish an errand. Her worry is of no value to her daughter and is only a hindrance to the mother herself. As her daughter sets out on an errand that can't be avoided, let her sit back in her chair, induce the relaxed state and picture on her imaginary screen her daughter arriving safely where she's going, while she herself remains in a state of serenity. It also offers a good opportunity to administer a posthypnotic suggestion to this effect:

"When I emerge from this state, I will find that I feel tranquil and content, being quite positive that all will be well with Mary Alice, that she'll walk in peace and reach her destination safely. I will go on about my chores and pleasures here in the house in a state of comfort and self-possession, feeling composed and placid, quite secure in the knowledge that my little girl will complete the necessary errand successfully."

Such imagery and posthypnotic implants indicate how the reader may use the technique to assuage his own worries over the well-being of someone close to him.

So many people today overreact to the hectic times in which we live. They pick up the tempo and the concerns of the people around them and grow nervous when the situation itself doesn't call for it. "I have to run now," they say, a phrase likely to be just as apt literally as figuratively. They run to work, run to the store, run to school. They seem to be on an accelerating carousel, going round and round and getting

nowhere—but getting there faster. Doctors have been warning us for years to slow down and live a little, lest we suffer the
consequences and arrange to live not at all. We hear the
warning but fail to heed it; maybe we're too busy running.

What's to give? The pace isn't likely to slow—more likely it
will quicken. If he tries to keep up, the individual in the
twentieth century unquestionably will be forced to pay an
escalating toll in coronaries, strokes, ulcers, nervous disorders
and other stress-induced ailments—possibly even cancer—to
say nothing of an exhausted zest for living and senses
deadened to the world around him.

But the two—both the pace *and* the pleasure of life—can be
made to coexist, not in a state of alternating power but in true
harmony. By pausing from time to time to reenergize the
human power plant through self-hypnosis, and in so doing
discharge enervating stress and strain, we may actually learn
to do more while enjoying it more.

Let's take a situation that most of us experience daily: getting to work. It may be by bus, train or subway, being swept
along by the rush-hour tide, jammed into an overcrowded car,
then jostled and bounced about until you reach your stop. Or
it may be in your own automobile out on the highway in
bumper-to-bumper, stop-and-go traffic, with horns blaring
and people shouting. Whatever the mode of transportation,
so much tension can build up that people arrive at their
destinations feeling as if they've already put in their full work-
day.

To avoid being one of the frazzled multitude, the night
before your journey induce the relaxed state, then engage in a
bit of imagery. As you walk to the train or bus, for example,
and you see the people around you quicken their steps and
grow excited, you move along calmly at a normal pace and
observe, "Well, that's their problem." When you board the
train or bus and take a seat or find standing space, you seem
unaffected by the grumbling and growling and smouldering
that other people are engaging in. Immune from it all, you
remark to yourself, "That person on the screen, namely me, is

in a state of self-control and self-command. My quietude and peace of mind remain firm as all of this hustle and bustle swirls around me."

At your destination (in your wall-imagery) you observe people pushing, yanking and snarling as they try to squeeze out the door, while you remain tranquil and in charge of yourself. You like the feeling and congratulate yourself on it. It would appear that as the tension of the people around you grows sharper, your muscles seem to get more relaxed, and you say to yourself, "The closer I get to the moment of crisis, the more calm, comfortable, serene and cool I feel."

Whether to surmount a critical situation or simply to cope with frenetic times, we will benefit further if—after our self-picturing and before terminating self-hypnosis—we will engage in a posthypnotic thought along these lines:

"When I emerge from this state I will find that my mood will be quiet and positive. I will feel in charge of myself and master of the situation, whatever it might be, and I will move in that state of quiet, composed comfort effectively and ably through the rest of the day."

CHAPTER 8

How to Control Physical Complaints

Let us turn now to the practical application of hypnosis to treat such physical negatives as pain and colds and sleeplessness. Unfortunately, few of us can simply snap our fingers and rid ourselves of whatever ails us. We need something extra, a technique that keys into our minds as well as our bodies. To command the body to behave in a way different from the way it habitually operates usually requires some additional know-how. One of the prime techniques we will be using in this process of gaining mastery over physical complaints is one of distraction. So simple and yet so potent! Nature has contrived that we concentrate effectively on a single subject at a time; we may be peripherally aware of other things, but we focus our attention on just one. It follows, therefore, that if we attend to pleasure, for instance, we shut out pain.

What happens when a child falls, scrapes a knee and starts to scream? If it's a little girl, we distract her attention from the injury to get her mind off it. We may enthusiastically admire the dress she's wearing or excitedly inspect a flower growing nearby. Miraculously, tears and crying subside as she ignores the pain and focuses attention on the distracting object.

This truth is crucial: we are what we think, we are what we picture, we are what we perceive. If these thoughts, pictures and perceptions are self-damaging ones, we can reverse their effect by distracting ourselves from the negative and focusing on the positive. This means we never mention the negative. In avoiding the concept "Don't," we refrain from saying "I will not feel pain," "I will not hiccup," "I will not lie sleepless all night." Again, it is like trying not to think of a purple elephant, which of course will summon the beast like lightning.

Confidence in positive behavior is further strengthened if we continue to remind ourselves that we have the ability to live with comfortable body feelings, that it is within our own power to live either well or poorly. We deceive ourselves into thinking that we are helpless little leaves in the wind. Many of us live that way, blown about by external events and by other people. But it isn't necessary to live so passively, and it certainly isn't desirable.

Let me reemphasize that rooting out one difficulty will not encourage another to grow in its place. It just isn't true that by eliminating a headache you will get a stomach ache. This superstitious barnacle has adhered to hypnosis for all too many years, giving people an excuse to avoid this sound approach to self-betterment. Our method of distraction to bring about mastery is designed not just to avoid the substitution of some such negative but actually to bring about an entire set of positives. As we have pointed out before, this has been the finding: as you conquer a habit or a bent toward self-destruction, success seems to ripple out and to increase health in all respects. People may doubt this; all we suggest is that they try it.

Pain

The first essential point to understand in the matter of using hypnosis to control pain is this:

In no sense do we intend to take the place of medicine. The technique we're offering here is designed to stand alongside, not to supplant, medical treatment. Pain is a signal that something is not right with the body. If you're experiencing pain, if you feel ill or if you have the slightest suspicion that something may be wrong physically, your first priority should be to lay down this book and reach for the telephone to call a physician. Let him or her give you clearance that there is no organic source to your complaint—or that there *is* and begin treating it medically. Only then should you attempt to practice hypnosis for pain relief, for its purpose and function is to treat the symptom—pain—not the cause of that pain.

Hypnosis can be used to reduce and sometimes even to eliminate the hurt caused by an infected tooth, but it won't cure the infection itself. Put another way, hypnosis does not remove pain; it removes the feeling of pain. This, of course, can be very helpful, because it leaves us feeling better. However, it can also be deceptive by masking the organic cause of the pain. "I feel fine now," you might be tempted to say. "I don't have to worry about that leg pain I used to have." Let your doctor determine whether you have anything to be concerned about.

There is also something to be said for consulting a hypnotherapist where pain is concerned. You are moving into territory that is rather uncharted in your life, but heavily charted by those people who have engaged in and teach self-hypnosis. If you want to make certain that you're on the right course, it may be fruitful to spend an hour with an expert in this approach. You may obtain the name of such a person in your area from either of the two organizations listed at the end of Chapter 1.

For now, let us assume that you have consulted a physician and he or she either has found no physical basis for your complaint or has found an organic source and is treating it. In either case, you want to rid yourself of pain. So, bear in mind the following premises:

(1) Self-hypnosis succeeds by shifting our awareness.

(2) Though pain may exist, we can filter out the hurt by shifting our awareness away from it. For example, have you ever experienced forgetting a sprained ankle or throbbing thumb while watching an exciting movie? That's just what we're proposing here: by seeing an absorbing movie unreel in our minds we can "forget" the pained part of the body.

(3) You have the capacity to shift your attention from pain to any scene you like.

With these premises in mind, we move to the self-hypnosis itself. First, induction of the relaxed state in the usual way. Then a syllogism, consisting of these three parts:

"For my body, not for me but for my body, attention to pain is a heavy burden.

"I need to feel light and comfortable to enjoy life.

"To the degree that I want to enjoy life, I will direct my attention to ———."

To fill that blank the self-hypnotist first verbalizes the scene in the syllogism, then pictures it in his mind's eye. If the distracting scene he shifts his attention to emerges from his own life, the image is in congruence with the way his organism works. It's best if the individual just turns his imagination loose and chooses the first scene that comes to mind that suits him. I happen to enjoy visualizing myself floating over the city in a balloon, but that image may frighten *you* to death. Select your own.

Perhaps you have a backache, in which case you may want to picture yourself floating on your back in blue Caribbean waters, feeling light and calm and pleasant. Maybe you want to direct your attention away from the pain of a cut finger. You might see yourself thrusting it into frigid ice water, numbing the finger to any sensation at all.

Suppose you want to rid yourself of a splitting headache. (My Aunt Minnie never had a simple headache; she always had a "splitting" headache.) Picture yourself setting a large block of ice with a hat-shaped hole in it over your head, a perfect fit. You feel some light tingling as that ice cools and numbs the entire head, and you find yourself sighing, "Ah, that feels good."

Or consider the scene envisioned by a woman about to give birth. Her obstetrician asked her, "Where would you rather be than on the delivery table?" She thought a moment and answered, "I'd like to be in the position that made me pregnant." If making love is *your* preferred scene, fine—there's nothing wrong with that. Picture it!

Your imagery may relate directly to the afflicted area, but not necessarily so. You may have a toothache. Where would you rather be than here suffering—fishing at some clear mountain stream, eagerly pulling in bass after bass? Or there was the patient who, when asked by her dentist, "What would you most like to be doing instead of sitting in my dental chair?" responded, "Frankly, I'd like to be doing housework; that's what I most enjoy." That's why we emphasize making the imagery uniquely your own, for only you know what you like to do best.

So it goes for a legion of aches and pains. You "forget" your pain by imagining yourself elsewhere. The little child pretending that he is captain of the *Queen Elizabeth II* gets so carried away in his imagination that he fails to hear his mother calling him to dinner. Become a child again. Pretend that something very pleasant is happening to you. On that imaginary white screen on the wall, or simply in your mind's eye, *see* it happening and *feel* it happening. Make it definite and make it vivid; keep doing so while ignoring all else.

After the visualizing stage of your self-hypnosis, the implantation of self-hypnotic suggestions is extremely important. Tell yourself that upon emergence you will feel at most a pressure in the area where you have been experiencing pain. "I may feel pressure," you can say to yourself. "I may feel a kind of tingle, perhaps a numbness. Apart from that I will feel light and comfortable. I will direct my thoughts toward pleasant things. I'm going to feel peaceful. I'll find myself enjoying better and better health as the hours pass."

And you emerge from the relaxed state in the usual way.

This method of relieving pain can be especially helpful to people who have an incurable bodily ailment. It has been widely assumed that the person who has terminal cancer, for example, must live in a state of either constant pain or drugged mental stupor. Studies have proved that this is not true. It is possible for the person who has an incurable disease to live it through in a state of relative ease and dignity. With this technique of distracting himself through self-hypnosis, such a person can shift his awareness and deny the painful

part of that illness. It would seem to be worth a good try for
such a person if there is the opportunity to make his life so
much more tolerable.

A colleague in hypnotherapy, Dr. Peter Wolf of Allen-
town (Pa.) General Hospital, treated such a patient, a woman
dying of cancer. He asked her the scene she would prefer
in her imagery. A Catholic, she said she would love to be
in the quiet and comfort of St. Paul's Church. So Dr. Wolf had
her imagine that she was in the church, walking down the aisle
toward the altar and pausing at a row of candles. He had her
take a candle, in her imagination, and let the wax drip down to
cover her hand. The hand grew quite numb. Then she would
pour the wax over her whole arm and over any other afflicted
part of the body, and where the wax fell she would feel nothing. To her understandably great relief the imagery worked.
The power of altered thinking had enabled her to filter out
the hurt from her pain.

The benefits of self-hypnosis in pain relief are often dramatic. I once heard a Boston physician give a first-person account of a genital operation performed without chemical
anesthesia, during which a sharp instrument was inserted in
his penis. He had hypnotized himself prior to the operation
and felt only pressure during it. In fact, he spent much of the
time soothing the incredulous and worried nurses. When the
operation was over, he climbed off the table, walked to his
hospital room, rested for a few hours, got out of bed, dressed
and went home.

The medical literature offers equally remarkable stories.
Dr. Milton H. Erickson has studied literally thousands of hypnotic subjects during his four decades of research. In his book,
Advanced Techniques of Hypnosis and Therapy, he reports on
many, representative of which is the case of Joe, a man termi-
nally ill with cancer.

"Upon inspecting Joe," Dr. Erickson writes, "it was noted
that much of the side of his face and neck was missing because of surgery, ulceration, maceration and necrosis. A
tracheotomy had been performed on Joe and he could not
talk. . . . every 4 hours Joe had been receiving narcotics (¼

grain of morphine or 100 milligrams of Demerol) and heavy sedation with barbiturates." Increased medication had led to toxic reactions, and Dr. Erickson had been called in to try to ease Joe's intense pain through hypnosis. In short, that's just what happened, and instead of spending his final days in a narcotic daze, Joe was able to go home with his family and remain alert, with aspirin the prescribed medication for any discomfort he felt.

"The symptom amelioration, abatement and actual abolishment effected by hypnosis," Dr. Erickson concludes, "and the freedom of Joe's body from potent medication, conducive only of unawareness, unquestionably increased his span of life while at the same time permitting an actual brief physical betterment in general. . . . Joe undertook to live the remainder of his life as enjoyably as possible, with a vigor expressive of the manner in which he had lived his life and built his business."

The inference should not be drawn that everyone would experience seemingly miraculous results, yet virtually everyone would reap at least some physical benefit from hypnosis. As explained by Harold J. Wain, director of the psychiatric liaison service at Walter Reed Army Medical Center in Washington (reported in *Science News,* October 30, 1976), "Every patient gets the minimal amount of relief. If you give a person relaxation, pain will be decreased as well." And, of course, relaxation is an integral part of self-hypnosis. An indication of the gains made by hypnosis in medical practice in the military is the fact that the technique is used on the majority of cases in the pain clinic at Walter Reed.

Some researchers believe that hypnosis, in addition to making the patient more comfortable, also hastens healing. *Prevention* magazine (July 1976) reported a meeting of the American Association for the Advancement of Science, remarking that a symposium on hypnosis "during one of the top scientific meetings of the year reinforces its acceptance by the scientific community as a potent therapeutic tool."

Speaking at the symposium, Dr. Kay F. Thompson, a dentist with the University of Pittsburgh School of Dental Medicine, stated, "I can't decide whether hypnosis promotes healing because there's a lack of pain, or whether pain interferes with healing when there's no hypnosis. But either way, the patient is helped."

Hypnosis has also been of demonstrable help in childbirth. Dr. William S. Kroger in 1957 performed the world's first Caesarean and also the first hysterectomy with hypnosis. Dr. R. L. August, a long-time practitioner and advocate of the technique, wrote of the superiority of hypnosis over chemical anesthesia in both ordinary childbirth and Caesarean section in his book, *Hypnosis in Obstetrics.*

Obstetricians using hypnosis have reported that (1) chemicals have an unfavorable effect on many babies, (2) with hypnosis the mother experiences greater comfort before, during and after the delivery, (3) the patient can walk from the operating room, (4) better and quicker breast-feeding results when the chemical anesthesia has been replaced by hypnosis, and (5) amazingly, less blood loss may occur when hypnosis is employed.

If in recent years hypnosis has earned increased respect in Western medical circles, it still has not achieved the status of a similar technique in Eastern culture, that of acupuncture. Indeed, the practice of sticking needles into the body to induce anesthesia is considered by many Western experts to be the Oriental equivalent of what we call hypnosis.

An interesting experiment comparing the anesthetic effects of hypnosis and of acupuncture was performed by John A. Stern, a psychologist at Washington University in St. Louis, and Dr. George A. Ulett, a psychiatrist. The test involved hypnosis, acupuncture with conventional needle sites, acupuncture with insertion sites selected at random, morphine, a tranquilizer, and a placebo.

The results, as reported by the *New York Daily News* (November 19, 1976): "The tranquilizer, the placebo and acupuncture at false points did not reduce pain. Hypnosis was the most effective pain killer. Acupuncture and morphine came in second."

And finally, before moving on to other disorders in the

physical category, a brief quotation reflecting two divergent roles self-hypnosis has played in pain control. In *Self-Hypnosis and Scientific Self-Suggestion,* W. J. Ousby, an English hypnotherapist, writes:

"During recent years, both in Britain and America, soldiers have been trained by using self-hypnotic techniques to render themselves immune from pain and even to undergo torture without betraying military secrets. The self-hypnotic trance is undoubtedly the secret which enables firewalkers and fakirs to perform their feats."

Allergies and Colds

In the previous discussion we deferred to medical experts to determine the *cause* of and to treat persistent pain. Similarly with allergies, we would yield to deeper methods of therapy than self-hypnosis in order to uncover the *source* of such symptoms as sneezing, itching, watering eyes, etc.

An allergy may be rooted in an infancy experience unremembered by the sufferer. It may be temporarily stemmed, but if it continues to return in spite of repeated efforts at self-hypnosis, then we hypothesize that the trouble is deeply entrenched, and some uncovering technique such as psychoanalysis (my preference) would be called for to insure complete and permanent relief.

We know that suggestion can influence one's allergic reactions. To test this hypothesis, Sarbin and Slagle carried out an experiment in Japan (reported in the Fromm-Shor book, *Hypnosis, Research Developments and Perspectives* [1972]). There were thirteen subjects, all of whom were allergic to the poisonous leaf of the Japanese wax tree, but not sensitive to chestnut-tree leaves. All thirteen subjects were blindfolded and told that one arm was being touched with the poisonous wax-tree leaf and the other arm with the harmless chestnut leaves. In actuality, just the reverse was done. But merely *believing* they had been exposed to a poisonous leaf caused all the subjects to show dermatitis on the arm touched by the nonallergenic chestnut leaves, while only one subject had an allergic reaction on the arm actually touched by a wax-tree leaf.

Many medical people hold that allergies do have a physical origin—pollen, dander, dust, etc.—and must be treated chemically. I'm not deterred by that view. As we have seen, the pain emanating from a knife cutting into one's flesh during surgery undoubtedly has a physical basis, yet hypnosis can divert the patient away from his physical pain so that all he feels is pressure. So, too, with allergies. Even if the affliction is not psychosomatic in nature and is caused by the invasion of the body by some external, foreign substance, we can still lessen the symptoms—the sneezing and sniffling, the itching and watering—with self-hypnosis. As you read earlier in this chapter, where hypnosis is used in childbirth less blood may occur. Obviously something happens *physically* when the patient is distracted from his physical difficulty. If bleeding can be lessened, isn't it likely that moisture in the nose, head and throat can likewise be diminished? Try it.

To do so, the person so afflicted would begin by relaxing his body, and then would envision a peaceful scene, followed by the mental recitation of a syllogism:

"For my body, not for me but for my body, these head symptoms are a poison.

"I need my body to live.

"To the degree that I want to live, I will protect my body as I would protect [name of loved one]."

With this verbal foundation, one then visualizes an image of oneself standing or sitting tall, serene, self-possessed. This person is in total command of brain and body, vibrant, strong and vigorous—in other words, the picture of health.

Then go on to implants. While in the state of heightened concentration and relaxation say to yourself, "I have the power, if I so choose, to live through this day symptom-free. I am in charge of my body. I will tell it when to sneeze and when not to sneeze. I will tell that nose when to get stuffed up. 'Go ahead, nose, get stuffed up. All right, nose, stop getting stuffed up.' I will declare my mastery over the body."

It is estimated that up to 75 percent of human ills have psychosomatic rather than physical bases. The most frequent of these human ailments is the common cold, which is blamed for more days lost from school or work than any other cause. Is it possible that an individual can arrange, perhaps unconsciously, to come down with a cold in order to avoid work or school? I submit that it is. To turn the matter around, I also believe that we have it within ourselves to remain relatively cold-free or, at any rate, largely symptom-free, if the body should be invaded by germs. Studies have shown that streptococcal infections, for example, are several times more frequent after periods of stress than during periods of tranquillity, so at the very least the serenity resulting from the practice of self-hypnosis would seem to render the body less hospitable to foreign bodies.

To illustrate this point, it has been my custom to tell patients that they have a right to get colds if they want, that they have a right to suffer, but to see it as *self-induced* suffering. One morning a patient came in sniffling and sneezing. "Last night," he recounted, "I felt this coming on, and I asked myself, 'Do I want this cold or don't I?' On other occasions I've said, 'No, I don't,' and decided I don't want to suffer, and so avoided it. But last night I just said, 'I think I'd like a cold tomorrow; I'll wake up with it.'" He wanted to baby himself and be nursed and feel a little sorry for himself for a while, so he opted for a cold.

The handling of colds is similar to that of allergies. Such negative thoughts as "Gee, it's drafty in this room" or "I feel a little sniffly; I wonder if I'm getting a cold" must be scotched immediately. And while you have the alternative of rushing to the medicine chest for an antihistamine, a more effective, more natural way of handling it is to induce the relaxed state. Next, picture that peaceful scene and remind yourself of the syllogism that for your body, any invasion by foreign substances is poisonous, that you need your body to live, and therefore that you will, in a decision to live, protect your body.

You may then visualize yourself in an atmosphere where you are symptom-free. You might even see yourself in an oxygen chamber, where one inhales only pure oxygen. You take breath after deep breath of that clear, clean element, firmly in control of your own breathing.

Insomnia

Why does a person have trouble sleeping? For one of three main reasons:

(1) The individual is troubled by some event in his life that keeps intruding. While his mind turns the matter over and over, he lies sleepless.

(2) Ironically, his fear of not being able to sleep keeps him from sleep. It's like fear of not having an erection: the negative takes over, supplanting the positive that is sought. How can you have an erection if you're distracted into the negative concern of fear? Thus, it may be said that any fear tends to bring about the event that is feared.

(3) External noises and happenings constitute a distracting influence. A patient said to me the other day, "Would you close the window, so I won't hear that dog barking?" I then became aware that there *was* a dog barking. Until then I had been distracted from the negative dog to the positive aspect of helping my patient, while he was distracted from the positive matter of achieving gains in his analysis into the negative preoccupation with a barking dog.

So, allowing a full night's sleep is a matter of distracting oneself away from these three deterrents—internal thoughts and emotions, fear of not sleeping, and external events and noises—toward the positive goal of sleep. We're assuming that previous efforts of exercising will power to get to sleep have proven fruitless.

Sleep and hypnosis, you may recall, are separate and distinct states but are members of the same family. It's easy to slip from hypnosis into sleep; hypnosis, like sleep, begins with a relaxing of the body. What is sleep but relaxation carried a step further to where concentration slips away entirely? The difference, of course, is that while both are relaxed states, hypnosis is a state of *raised* concentration, and sleep, by its very nature, is *reduced* concentration. Paradoxically, by concentrating on sleep we lose the ability to concentrate on anything at all as the mind slips into the sleep state.

The would-be sleeper begins by giving special attention to relaxing his body, employing a technique such as the Jacobson method of progressive muscle relaxation described in Chapter 5. After such an exercise the muscles may be generally relaxed, but most likely the mind is not relaxed. To put the mind to rest we begin with the customary induction: roll up the eyes; with the eyes gazing up, slowly lower the lids; take a deep breath; hold it; relax the eyes and let the body float.

Now float deeper and deeper into the bed. There's something very pleasant and peaceful about this floating, and as you sink deeper into the relaxed state, picture your favorite scene of tranquillity. I've mentioned mine: a Caribbean beach. One of my patients envisions a garden with a splashing fountain and beautiful flowers. Another says that he feels most comfortable when he's lying in bed just after intercourse, so that's what he imagines. Whatever your favorite scene, invoke it, then say to yourself, "It's easy to shift from my present state into sleep." Many people will find that just by reminding themselves of that fact, they will go to sleep.

If you do not, we go on to a very simple exercise. We count every inhalation, and with every exhalation we think the word "sleep." Thus (inhale) "one," (exhale) "sleep," (inhale) "two," (exhale) "sleep," (inhale) "three," (exhale) "sleep," etc. Throughout, we continue to float. We have now distracted ourselves from pains, worries, fears and noises—all of these negatives—to the positive subject of sleep. We continue counting up to ten. Many people find that they don't reach ten. But if you do, don't let that trouble you. Start all over and do it once again. If you're among the few who go through a second ten, try a third. Eventually sleep will occur.

You may notice that we've omitted a syllogism in this procedure to induce sleep. It seems to me superfluous in this case, and I myself leave out the syllogism when I engage in the exercise routinely every night. If you would feel more comfortable with one, however, recite it before the counting exercise, incorporating the concept that "wakefulness is a poison."

Some people find that they fall asleep easily enough, but then wake in the night and lie sleepless. I would suggest to them that upon retiring they induce their self-hypnosis and then give themselves a simple posthypnotic implant such as "I will slip easily from my present state into the sleep state, and after I do, I will sleep soundly and steadily through the night."

If practiced successfully there will be no need to bring yourself out of the relaxed state—your psychic sleeping position will have delivered you to Morpheus.

Tiredness (Fatigue)

There are people who say that even though they get enough sleep at night, they still feel tired and listless during the day and can't dredge up the energy to do much of anything. The weight of the world seems to rest on their weary shoulders—they're Atlases with tired blood.

After inducing the relaxed state, the chronically tired individual mentally states a syllogism:

"For my feelings of well-being, fatigue is harmful, even ruinous.

"I need my feelings of well-being in order to live in a state of comfort.

"To the degree that I want to live comfortably, I'll allow surges of strength to flow through my body."

It's then easy to go on to the visualizing. You imagine yourself at a favorite site—let's say at the side of a lake—infused now with new strength and stamina. You feel an urge to rise from your chair, stretch, send your shoulders back and expand your chest. You feel yourself growing stronger and stronger, filled with a desire for physical activity. Depending on your preference, you then strip and jump into the water, run around the lake or do a headstand, all the time enjoying a state of increasing energy, exulting in it and saying, "I feel strong; I feel vigorous; I feel able."

And then you emerge from the induced state.

Engaged in several times a day, this self-treatment for increased strength will bring results. You are talking to your muscles, telling them to come alive. At your direction, they will obey.

Hiccups

Sometimes a patient who can't stop the hiccups comes in. He may complain that he has been hiccupping this way for twenty-four hours or more, that it has kept him from sleeping, other than just dozing, and has interfered with his eating and other activities. Or someone in therapy will complain that occasionally he'll get a spell of hiccupping that will go on for an hour or so, and while it doesn't interfere with sleep or eating, it can be both a nuisance and an embarrassment. He'd like to eliminate or at least reduce such episodes.

The person prone to hiccup attacks should begin his treatment by inducing the state of self-hypnosis. After he has done so and is floating deeper and deeper into his chair, calm and comfortable, and when he senses that he is muscularly, emotionally and mentally released, he may engage in this kind of syllogism:

"This involuntary hiccupping means my body is out of control and in disequilibrium.

"I need my equilibrium and feeling of self-control in order to live comfortably.

"To the degree that I want to live comfortably, I'll breathe smoothly and rhythmically."

Then, as you continue in your raised state, engage in the customary visualizing. See yourself, on your imaginary screen, sitting quite calmly, talking to someone else, watching television, or eating—all the while breathing rhythmically. Or you may visualize yourself walking along the street, alive to the people and the scene around you, breathing normally and feeling quite content and comfortable.

Before emerging from the raised state, employ an appropriate posthypnotic suggestion, *e.g.,* "Between now and sleep time my breathing will tend to be steady, easy and smooth."

Itching

You have an itch. Your scratching at it has produced ugly red streaks and splotches. You're annoyed with it and with yourself, and you want it to stop. What do you do? First, you bring about the induced state. Second, you remind yourself that:

"Not for me but for my body, this itch is damaging; it means my body is out of control.

"To live comfortably, I need control over my body.

"To the degree that I wish to live comfortably, I will itch at my decision and at the body location of my choosing."

Here you are assuming mastery over your body. Tell yourself that if your right elbow is itching you will produce an itch on your left knee. The itch on your right elbow means your body is out of control, but an itch at your decision means your body is in control. Today you choose control and will itch on your left knee. This is an approach wherein the shifting of attention elsewhere is of great use.

You then see yourself, in your mind's eye, sitting in your living room chair and looking at your left knee, which begins to itch. Continue to concentrate on that itching left knee, reminding yourself that *you* brought about that itch and that your body is in *your* control. You will find that you will be so distracted from your right elbow that the undesired itch just will not be there.

So distracted, you bring yourself out of your self-hypnosis.

Asthma

The asthmatic's handling of his ailment is no different from anyone else's in this chapter. After inducing the relaxed state, he gives himself a syllogism focusing on his particular asthmatic symptom, which may be frequent sneezing, a filled nose, clogged throat or shortness of breath. It can be in any part of the head or chest, and it can be felt either as pain or simply as a nuisance. The asthmatic will cast the opening term of the syllogism in accordance with whatever's bothering him:

"For my body, not for me but for my body, this sneezing [or whatever the difficulty] is heavily burdensome.

"I need to feel light and comfortable in order to enjoy life.

"To the degree that I want to enjoy life, I will direct my attention to ————."

He fills that blank with his favorite locale where he can breathe easily and freely, perhaps a mountaintop or desert. He next visualizes himself at the site of this ideal atmosphere, breathing in that pure, clear air. It feels so pleasant and comfortable to be there. Then, before terminating his self-hypnosis, he gives himself a posthypnotic suggestion to this effect: "When I emerge from this state I will find that with each succeeding breath my breathing will become easier and easier."

Does it really work? Try it and see.

CHAPTER 9

How to Overcome Sexual Difficulties

For whatever reasons, people tend to cloak their sexual problems in shame and zealously conceal them from others—sometimes from themselves, as well. Nobody really knows the extent of sexual dysfunction among the human population, but we do know that troubles relating to sex motivate more people to seek aid from marriage counselors and psychotherapists than any other single cause. Furthermore, it is safe to say that virtually everyone at some time in his adult life is going to experience sexual malfunctioning; for some, it is a distressing daily companion for long periods, even for a lifetime.

The bumpy road to sexual health can be long and even arduous. Since problems in the adult bed commonly trace their beginnings to the cradle, extensive therapy frequently is found necessary before the individual begins to function well sexually. The process can be time-consuming and expensive, and for these reasons, among others, countless people who could benefit from psychotherapy for their sex problems simply do not receive it.

For some of these people—not for everyone, but certainly for some—self-hypnosis can help. Workers in the field use hypnosis to treat a variety of sexual difficulties, and success has ranged from zero to spectacular. The eminent Dr. Lewis R. Wolberg has flatly stated, "Sexual difficulties seem to clear up rapidly in hypnotherapy, often without relapse."

I myself can report numerous successes, some of which will be discussed in this chapter, as well as some failures. There is just no way of telling in advance whether and to what extent self-hypnosis might work for you to clear up sexual troubles. My advice, obvious by now, is to give it a full college try.

Just how long is a full college try? I would suggest practicing the exercise several times a day for a period of three weeks. After that period of conscientious performance, if there are absolutely no results, no amelioration of the symptom or condition, then you may be fairly sure there is some information about your psyche and its early history that needs professional attention to unearth. On the other hand, many people will find that self-hypnosis alone will bring the results they seek. Trying it is the only way of determining in which camp you belong.

Now for some specific complaints.

Low Sexual Urge

One area where self-hypnosis has been quite successfully employed is in helping people with reduced sexual interest to spark their desire for sexual activity. I'd like to present the story of Louise as a case in point.

A thirty-year-old mother of two, Louise described how she felt about sexual intercourse with her husband Richard: "I give my husband excuses that I don't feel well or that I'm tired, but actually I'm just not interested. Sometimes I have to let him make love to me, and it's okay, but I'm still glad when it's all over."

We learned upon questioning that ten years previously, while on their honeymoon, Louise had experienced pain during intercourse. Medical examination revealed tumors on an ovary, which was removed. Surgery successfully eliminated both the cause of pain and the pain itself, but from then on, she lost all interest in sex.

Since there is little or no evidence that the removal of an ovary, or for that matter an entire hysterectomy, should lead to a reduction in sexual drive, the explanation for Louise's lack of sexual desire had to reside in her head, not elsewhere in her anatomy. If we go on that assumption, we take the further step of observing that perhaps the remembered sensation of pain is now blocking out sexual pleasure.

So we enter hypnosis with this theory—that the memory of pain was turning Louise off just as the actual pain had done ten years earlier. We design a syllogism to frame the pain memory in the context of self-arranged damage, which it is, and then we will provide a new positive mental image to supplement that framework. First, the syllogism:

"For the success of my marriage, acting as if a vaginal pain that vanished ten years ago were still bothering me is ruinous.

"I need a successful marriage in order to live happily.

"To the degree that I want to live happily, I'll allow myself to enjoy love-making."

Unlike Louise, you may not be aware of a negative history that is holding you back, in which case, consider the following syllogism:

"For the success of my relationship, sexual indifference is ruinous.

"I need a successful relationship in order to live happily.

"To the degree that I want to live happily, I'll allow myself to enjoy love-making."

Then the visualizing. While still in the relaxed state, see yourself on your imaginary white screen, in the bedroom with your partner. Look at him or her fondly, imbued with feelings of caring, of tenderness, of wanting to touch and be touched. See yourself approach your partner as he or she approaches you; you meet and embrace. Your mind then carries you right through the act of love, preceded by whatever foreplay you wish, and all of it accomplished in an airy, floating, pleasant and accepting frame of mind.

This is the idea to amplify and embellish: that it is a rich, happy experience that you look forward to eagerly and that you see happening in all its joyful rapture. Do all you can, in your picturing, to make it a full, rewarding, comfortable happening.

Then you may give yourself a posthypnotic suggestion to the effect that the event in reality will be a positive and pleasurable one, just as it was in your imagination. It will be as if you were on pillows or on air, feet scarcely touching the floor, body scarcely touching the bed. It's an exhilarating, heady feeling.

Finally, you bring yourself out of your self-hypnosis in the usual way.

The self-hypnosis performed before engaging in lovemaking advisedly includes the special relaxation exercises described in Chapter 5. As you progressively relax each part of the body, letting all the tension flow out, you induce a greater and deeper state of overall relaxation, thus allowing for a greater sense of release in bed.

Impotence

Most men experience brief episodes of impotence at one time or another, but the affliction soon passes. When impotence lasts for long periods or keeps returning with some regularity, a man understandably wishes to gain mastery over it. (In a paper in *The Conditioning Therapies: The Challenge in Psychotherapy,* Dr. A. Hussain tells of a man, married and impotent for ten years, who was cured by hypnosis. Dr. Hussain also reports on a study in which 95 percent of 105 patients with sexual difficulties were successfully treated with hypnosis.)

In my own practice, a representative case was that of Jack, a comptroller for a small manufacturing company in New Jersey. Jack and Doris had lived together harmoniously for two and a half years, despite the fact that during the first six months of their marriage Doris had added too many pounds, causing Jack's sexual interest to dwindle. Their sexual relations stopped entirely and, presumably to compensate, Jack stepped up his drinking and Doris her eating.

In my office, Jack recalled that his mother had been obese and that it had been her custom to throw dishware at his father when Jack was little, with Jack and his sister clinging to each other in terror. Our hypothesis was that in his mind Jack had linked the overweight Doris with his fat mother, thus rendering Doris as terrifying as his mother had been. With that insight, we devised this syllogism:

"For my marriage, fearing Doris as if she were my mother is a poison.

"I need my marriage in order to enjoy life.

"To the degree that I want to enjoy life, I will see Doris as the sweet, caring woman she actually is, wanting only to embrace her lovingly."

If you find yourself in the predicament of having either no erection or insufficient erection, and if you know of an event in your earlier life similar to Jack's, you can work your own history into the syllogism. If not, and without any deep self-study, you may construct your own syllogism for your particular needs. Perhaps the word "fear" seems inapplicable in your case—you don't sense that you fear your partner—so you may want to use a much more generic term, such as "distancing," in the syllogism:

"For my happy relationship, distancing myself from my partner is a poison.

"I need my happy relationship to enjoy life to the fullest.

"To the degree that I want to enjoy life, I will see my partner in a positive, loving way."

You may substitute any other term that seems appropriate to you for impotence: "keeping away from," "spurning," "separating myself from." The point is that there is a distancing: the genital organ is not reaching out for the other person; it's staying away.

I would suggest inducing self-hypnosis prior to intercourse. Then, following the syllogism, visualize the act of love happening comfortably, freely and successfully, almost as if you were floating on a cloud. Give yourself the posthypnotic suggestion that during actual love-making you will continue to float in the very same fashion as when you are in the altered condition of consciousness.

Tell yourself that the act of love to follow will be an easy, pleasurable thing, that you will want only to be close to and caress—and to be caressed by—your partner. There will be no demands, no obligations, just tender caring in a pleasurable, relaxed state.

So, in your conquest over impotence, you do three things:

(1) Point out to yourself in the syllogism that fear of or distancing yourself from your partner is harmful to your relationship and consequently to your full enjoyment of life.

(2) Visualize yourself coming together with your partner and accomplishing the act of love effortlessly and comfortably.

(3) In a posthypnotic suggestion, tell yourself that you will be doing this in quite an easy and floating fashion, with no requirements placed upon yourself. It will just happen in a relaxed frame of mind, comfortably and pleasurably.

Difficulty in Ejaculating

Let's consider the man who has no erection problem—in fact, just the opposite. He goes on and on during intercourse, and while his partner may be experiencing varying degrees of ecstasy, he remains on a plateau, unable to ejaculate.

In working toward a syllogism, it is helpful to see that in a sense he is holding back. If you asked him about it, he might deny it: "*I'm* not holding back; my organ is holding back." Well, his organ is part of him, so somewhere in his mind, I submit, he is withholding. His objective is to let go. Accepting that as the problem—and I think it doesn't take too much imagination to do so—he can then formulate the syllogism:

"For my present comfort [or for my relationship with my partner] this holding back is ruinous.

"I need to feel comfortable in order to enjoy love-making and to make the most of my relationship.

"To the degree that I want to make love successfully and have a full relationship, I will allow myself to release [or I will let myself go]."

After you have carved out the syllogism to fit your needs—and here I want to emphasize that you modify the situation and wording to suit *yourself,* not a hypothetical model—go on to the visualizing.

You begin by observing yourself, on your white screen, approaching your partner. You feel good about it, comfortable with it. You suffuse that figure on the screen, which is yourself, with feelings of wanting to enjoy and wanting to give. You watch the usual steps preparatory to love-making, then the act itself occurring in a state of easy floating. You relish her body and glory in it, while growing progressively more eager. Finally, you allow yourself a wish and an urge just to let go, to release yourself. You follow through, and it happens.

You will also give yourself a posthypnotic suggestion (either at this point or earlier; there's nothing rigid about the order) that whenever you actually engage in intercourse you are going to be floating in the same fashion in which you float while in self-hypnosis, and that this will lead to a satisfying release.

Following the visualizing and posthypnotic suggestion, you terminate the exercise.

Orgasmic Difficulty in Women

Similar to the man who can't ejaculate is the woman who fails to reach the final release known as climax. There is no lack of sexual interest that you're aware of. You want your man and you're excited by him, but you reach a certain peak and just stay there.

What's happening? Like the man who cannot ejaculate, you

are holding back. Are you afraid? Are you angry? Has there been an event in your life that has you feeling you must withhold release? Perhaps you can find such an incident. In any case, whether you can or not, you may be sure until it is proved otherwise that you are holding something back. You may examine your feelings to see whether you're frightened or angry or there's some other negative emotion that is making you withhold yourself. If there is, you can weave that right into your syllogism, i.e., any such anger or fear is a barrier to a happy relationship with your man.

But you may find nothing, which is often the case. The person just says, "I don't sense any emotion. I'm not afraid; I'm not annoyed with him; I love him and I want him. I just feel so helpless; nothing seems to happen." If this is the case, you can still mold your syllogism around such terms as "withholding," "holding back," "holding on," "not wanting to let go," etc. For that is what's happening on some level, even if you don't know the specific nature of the emotion inducing you to hold back. Your syllogism may then go something like this:

"For my comfort and well-being, this holding on that I'm engaging in is a barrier to a happy relationship with my man.

"I need this happy relationship in order to live fully and contentedly.

"To the degree that I want to live in contentment, I will allow myself to let go."

As with the man who doesn't ejaculate, the so-called frigid woman visualizes, in great detail, the act of love. It's a comfortable, easy, pleasant kind of experience. You linger on the happening, allowing yourself to feel increasingly peaceful, floating, increasingly confident that the culmination will occur.

There is no life-or-death situation here. There's really nothing to be gained by climax but your own release and pleasure; it releases tension and brings excitement and joy. That is all you're working toward—letting yourself enjoy. Your partner does not require (and you can have this understanding with him), nor do you require of yourself, that there be a climax. It's simply better that way. So picture it *being* better that way, and through the repeated application of this method, it can happen.

Before emerging from your self-hypnosis, you may give yourself the posthypnotic suggestion that you will float comfortably through the sexual act just as you float during the relaxed state, and that it will be similarly easy for you to let go.

A cautionary word: do not expect triumphant success on your first try. Fortunately, tomorrow is another night, so just keep at it, with the confidence that each time you engage in this kind of hypnotherapy you are chipping away at the hard rock of resistance, and release will eventually happen.

Premature Ejaculation

A disorder the woman doesn't have to be concerned about is having a premature climax. If she precedes the man, it's usually not difficult for her to continue in the act of love until he releases. But probably every man occasionally experiences a climax that is earlier than is wanted by either partner. However, it is the man who regularly ejaculates too soon that we are concerned with here. His providing too much too fast is a psychic matter, the reason for which lies somewhere in his early history. Premature ejaculation, like certain other complex sexual problems such as homosexuality, involves an infancy or childhood cause that usually calls for exploration. If you can find the reason for it yourself, excellent. If not, you may wish to consult someone who has had experience in unraveling these problems.

But you may have neither the time nor the money to seek out an expert and may want to treat the dysfunction yourself. Begin by trying some self-exploration to answer the question, "What might have happened early in my life that has me expressing anger at my partner, wanting to climax too soon so that she won't experience enjoyment?" This often lies behind premature ejaculation: the wish to deny your partner pleasure. But, ironically, you hurt yourself by keeping yourself from prolonging your pleasure. In this denial of yourself you have the basis for a syllogism:

"For my own enjoyment and for my relationship with my woman, my early climax is a self-denial.

"I need my own enjoyment and this relationship to live to the fullest.

"To the degree that I wish full enjoyment in the bedroom and in my relationship, I will find it easy to float in an erect state until maximum pleasure is experienced by both of us."

I would count heavily on visualizing here, seeing yourself on that imaginary wall screen as relaxed and comfortable, floating, thoroughly enjoying the sexual experience. Minutes go by as you assume all kinds of positions, your excitement kept at a middle, manageable level, never losing yourself. If it's helpful to keep your midsection away from your partner while exciting her in other ways, do so. Perhaps entry occurs at the moment you sense her climax beginning. The prolonged act of love will take place in a state of smiling satisfaction on your part, right up to the moment you give yourself the signal that you want it to terminate. You call the shots. You determine when your climax is to happen.

Then you give yourself the posthypnotic suggestion that only on a deliberate mental signal from you will ejaculation occur. Finally, you emerge from the relaxed state in the usual way. *Caution: it won't happen the first time.* And it might not happen the fourth time. But you're making progress. Each performance of this exercise brings you closer to your goal of mastery over the timing of your sexual release.

Homosexuality

Suppose you are a homosexual. You may be content with your sexual orientation—if so, fine. But if you *are* uncomfortable with it and wish to change, consider the use of self-hypnosis.

In this discussion, I'd like first to present the Case of the

Whipped Homosexual, that of a man who came to me for psychoanalysis. Fred, a court stenographer living in Philadelphia with his mother, was plagued by a homosexual fantasy in which a naked man forced Fred to kneel and then, standing over him, cursed Fred angrily as he flailed him with a horsewhip.

To speak of the analysis for a moment, these facts emerged: Fred came from an unhappy farm home where his father drank heavily and his mother bore children and complained constantly. The youngest of four children, Fred lived in constant fear of his father's anger and mean teasing by two older brothers. Mother also used him as a verbal target for her anger at his father and the other children.

Several months of analysis had managed to clear up a few ancillary problems connected with my patient's work and his getting along with colleagues, but had left his homosexuality intact. We turned then to hypnosis for treatment—first, hypnosis by the therapist (myself), and then self-hypnosis. I began by inducing hypnosis and regressing Fred to his early life at home. In reliving these childhood years, he quickly pinpointed two crucial memories.

The first was that his father often whipped his older brothers as Fred watched and quivered in fear. But the father never whipped Fred himself. The second memory was that when he was a naughty boy his mother would tell him, "All right, get the whip!" This was Fred's cue to go to the barn to fetch a whip that hung there and bring it to her. But she never used it on him—the threat was apparently enough to scare him out of any naughtiness he was engaged in.

After emerging from that regressed state, he told me that when he was about twelve years old, having taken all of this for years, he finally got an idea. He went out to the barn, took down the whip, went outside and threw it in the creek. "I realize now," he remarked, "how long it took me to get rid of the whip."

I commented dryly that his homosexual fantasy demonstrated that he never *had* given up the whip. It appeared to me that on some level Fred was "jealous" of his brothers' getting

those whippings, just as there was also a vacuum when his
mother failed to whip him. It was almost as if some part of him
yearned for this punishment (possibly to alleviate guilt for his
naughtiness).

Thus, through his adult fantasy he was living out a whipping that he somehow had wanted as a child and continued to
long for as an adult. Until brought out in hypnosis, it had
never occurred to him that he would have desired anything so
negative as whippings. The high level of concentration inherent in the hypnotic experience had enabled Fred to home in
on the key memory. Yes, such memories do come out in
analysis, but they often get lost in the panoramic sweep of a
personal history. Some patients, Fred included, are able to do
something in hypnosis that eludes them in the free association
of psychoanalysis: go right to the heart of the problem.

Armed with the vital information from Fred's childhood,
we fashioned a syllogism around it: that the entire whipping
fantasy was a poison to his emotional life. We further devised a
posthypnotic suggestion that he could get along without wanting to be whipped by either his father or his mother, that he
would no longer require whipping by the fantasy man, no
longer require the man's cursing, no longer require the man
himself. Furthermore, he would find that he could become
sexually aroused by a woman.

To race through subsequent events: Fred came in the following week and told me that he had faithfully gone into
self-hypnosis several times a day during that week and that the
man continued to stand over him and curse during his fantasies, but the whip had disappeared. The next week he reported that his self-hypnosis was continuing and that the
cursing had disappeared in his fantasy, along with the whip.
The week after that he announced that in his fantasy the man,
sans both whip and cursing, was now simply lying beside him
in bed.

This went on for a couple more weeks, whereupon Fred
told me that the man inhabiting his fantasy had become very
gentle, loving and kind, and that halfway through the fantasy,
unasked—not of his conscious bidding in any way—the man

had disappeared, and it was now a woman who was lying beside him. The man continued to intrude into his fantasy from time to time, but whenever he did, Fred could easily dispatch him by deliberately imagining the woman back. Eventually, encouraged by his progress in ordering his fantasy world and helped by further psychoanalysis, he was able to achieve similar results in reality.

In summary, hypnosis provided the key that unlocked the hidden memories attached to Fred's whipping fantasy, and through self-hypnosis he was able not only to eradicate the abhorrent fantasy, but to kindle a healthy interest in women as well.

As was the case with Fred, homosexuality usually calls for some exploration with in-depth therapy in addition to self-hypnosis. But again, there are no strictures. Since self-hypnosis is harmless, there is nothing to be lost in trying it. On the contrary, you may very well help yourself.

To use it for treating homosexuality, begin by writing yourself a syllogism. If you can find salient memory material as Fred did, so much the better. If not, something along these lines will serve quite well:

"To be attracted to a person of my own sex is to hamper my emotional life and my social life.

"I need a productive emotional life and social life in order to live contentedly.

"To the degree that I want to live contentedly, I will allow myself to reach out to a person of the opposite sex."

And then visualize it happening. There are behavioral therapists who administer minor shocks to a homosexual woman looking at a picture of another woman, or to a man looking at a man. That is aversive behavioral therapy designed to turn a person away from one of his own sex. If you wish to give yourself a mild shock in the form of feelings of distaste as you observe yourself looking at a person of your own sex, envision it so.

But my own preference is in favor of picturing the positive. Here your own imagination is the only bar to what you will see. You may visualize yourself on that imaginary white screen, coming out of your house or building, walking down the street and suddenly seeing an attractive person of the opposite sex. Or you may imagine that you attend a dance or party, look about you and see an interesting girl if you're a man, or a man if you're a woman. There is an exchange of glances, and you feel almost magnetically drawn to this person. You watch this happening, and you let the relationship develop. You see the various steps of courtship take place, progressing to the ultimate embrace.

The transition from "hello" to a sexual embrace is, to be sure, a gradual, step-by-step series of events. Therefore, allow yourself to see it all unfold in progressive fantasies, at your own pace, leading to culmination.

Before emerging from the relaxed state, give yourself the posthypnotic suggestion that on seeing an attractive person of the other sex you will feel a forward movement in yourself, a positive attraction toward that person.

All of this is within your capacity. You have the power. After several weeks of conscientious trial, several times a day, if you see no sign of change, but you really *want* to change, you should visit someone experienced in such matters.

On the other hand, if after days or even weeks of faithful practice, signals appear that indicate your sexual orientation might be shifting, you know that you're on the right track. Keep it up.

CHAPTER 10

Building Positive Feelings and Attitudes

In the chapters immediately preceding, we have been dealing for the most part with unwanted negatives and their elimination: harmful habits, emotional problems, physical complaints and sexual difficulties. We move now to the sunny side of the behavioral street, where we will "accentuate the positive."

It's true that many of these positives are merely the flip sides of their negative counterparts and that an efficient way of handling the positive is simply to eliminate its opposite; i.e., do away with procrastination, and you foster promptness; eradicate insomnia, and sound sleep results; drop body-damaging habits such as smoking or overeating, and better health is the consequence, etc. In other words, weed out the bad and in grows the good.

Another way of instilling healthy emotions, attitudes and practices is to devise a direct, methodological approach to affirming them. Such will be our objective in this chapter and the next: not to reverse behavior, but to improve or build upon your present foundation. We acknowledge that most people come to self-hypnosis for help in correcting something they don't like in themselves, and therefore we have given major emphasis in this book to correcting the negative. But let us assume you have smoothed out unwanted flaws in mind and body and now want to enhance the attributes you possess. We will seek to strengthen, through self-hypnosis, matters of the heart, head and hand, that is, emotions, attitudes and skills. Ways of sharpening mental and manual dexterity—skills— will be explored in Chapter 11, while we take up the matter of feelings and attitudes now.

Love and Warmth

One cluster of emotions, with love as the centerpiece, in- volves our caring about other people. Such warm feelings as sympathy, empathy, tenderness, affection, kindness and friendliness draw people together and therefore make living a richer experience. There are some people, either unwilling or unable to extend their feelings to others, who remain isolated. If they choose to live as emotional hermits, that is their privilege and in no way do we wish to appear critical of such a choice. This chapter is aimed instead at those individuals who wish they had more or stronger love feelings and who elect to do something about it.

Of course, some people have such feelings but are inhibited about letting them out. A man was saying to me recently, "I met this lovely girl, and I felt positive vibrations from her. I wanted so to get to know her, but somehow I felt all locked up inside." Let's concern ourselves here with unlocking these handcuffs, or "heartcuffs."

To do so, begin by inducing the relaxed state, as described earlier in this book. Then consider the elements of this syl- logism:

"For my favorable relations with others, to let myself feel the emotion of love is essential.

"I need favorable relations with others in order to live fully and comfortably.

"To the degree that I choose to live fully and comfortably, I'll allow myself to radiate the warmth of love."

It may be that "love" is a little strong for the relationship you want to establish with another. You may simply want to deepen your feelings of affection and warmth toward your friends, relatives and co-workers. You may wish just to feel friendlier toward a neighbor, a person in the community, a schoolmate or a colleague at work, but you find that friendly feelings are absent or are smothered by some aspect of envy, anger or hostility. In other words, your feelings are ambivalent: the friendliness you'd like to express is snuffed out by feelings of annoyance. You want to banish these negative emotions while expanding positive ones. You know that doing so will make *you* feel better and furthermore that it may be in your best interests to do so.

So, in the syllogism above, you substitute words like "friendliness," "kindness," "understanding," "acceptance" for the word "love." The same principle holds: you do need favorable relations with these people—the minister whose austere manner frightens you a little or the loud-talking person at the next desk—and so, to the degree you wish to live comfortably, you allow yourself to radiate the warmth of friendliness and kindness and acceptance.

The same would apply to such feelings as "affection" and "tenderness" toward a child or even a pet. Let's say a neighbor has a rather obstreperous offspring who treads on your toes—or your petunias—and therefore on your patience. Someone might tell you, "Look, if you would treat little Algernon there with more affection, he might leave your petunias alone." Thus, for you to let feelings of tenderness suffuse and supplant those of irritability might very well prove beneficial to both your state of mind and your petunia patch.

Our objective isn't intellectual here. Through the syllogism we're establishing a frame of mind, a mood that will help us extend our emotions toward other people. Having set up such a state of mind, we go to the customary visualization. Begin by casting onto an imagined screen on the wall a picture of yourself in relation to someone else.

There you are, a woman, let us say, meeting a man for the first time. You have heard favorable things about him and would *like* to like him, but somehow you're feeling nothing at all. In your visualizing, strive to make the intangible visible. *See* lines of emotional vibrations coming right out of your body, stretching across space and touching that man. These lines may be red or pink, or perhaps a rainbow of vibrating bands of color that connects you to him, each color terminating in an arrow that points right at the man. As you continue to express these feelings as bands of color, you notice that your face relaxes and its expression becomes warm and welcoming. In response, the man also lets down mental barriers, breaks into a smile and holds out his hand.

You witness your feelings of caring go out to him—whether they are feelings of love, friendliness or empathy and understanding—and see them expressed in your body line and in the way you're standing. You can't help moving a step toward him. You observe that as he feels your radiating feelings, he responds in kind. You can expand on this exchange as much as you like. Let your own imagination be your guide as to the extent of the harmony growing between you two.

You may envision a similar scene in regard to meeting several people. Imagine that you're being introduced to a group of possible employers and you're a little scared. You want to rid yourself of this negative emotion, knowing that these people might misinterpret your fear as hostility and therefore turn away from you. You want to feel friendly and as one with them.

Again, you simply visualize positive vibrations flowing from you to them. Your whole attitude is positive. Your body posture is in their direction; your feet are pointed toward them. Your hand reaches out and grasps another's hand; you smile, you radiate, you beam your friendliness. Likewise, you visualize the hearty response from the other people. They murmur in admiration of you; they praise you outright; they grin; they clap you on the back. Observe this; enjoy it.

Then give yourself the posthypnotic suggestion that when you emerge from this state, you will find that an aura of friendliness and easy affection will permeate your meeting with these people (or that person, as in the first situation). You will feel strongly positive toward the entire group (or toward that person), who in turn will respond positively to you. Once you have engaged in such visualizing and self-suggestion to your satisfaction, you emerge from this relaxed state in the usual fashion.

Another situation you might envisage is contact with strangers. These are the people you meet throughout the day—bus drivers, waitresses, fellow motorists, repairmen, etc.—whose lives you touch for a moment and whom you may not see again, like the proverbial ships that pass in the night. Rather than projecting antagonism or mistrust and turning within yourself, see yourself, as you walk down the street, as opening up, smiling and radiating warm, friendly feelings toward everyone you meet.

I remember a man who told me how amazed he was to discover the number of smiles he could elicit from strangers as he walked down Fifth Avenue in New York. After picturing yourself doing the same during your self-hypnosis, when you emerge it might be rewarding to go out on the street and see if the experiment reported to the therapist is replicable. You may find it exhilarating, as well as an eye- (and heart-) opening experience.

Good Humor

We may subsume another grouping of positive attitudes under the heading of contentment with oneself, as distinguished from the love feelings described above, which have to do with our relationships with others. In this group we will include such emotions and attitudes as good humor, cheerfulness, optimism and enthusiasm. For you and me to allow ourselves to feel in the "up" frame of mind suggested by these words is to feel content as we move through our days. If we have a choice between contentment and misery, as I hold that we do, then there's a great deal to be said for selecting the former: it's easier on us and also on those around us, who in turn react more favorably to us. Thus, good cheer has a self-benefiting boomerang effect.

Once again, after invoking the altered state of consciousness we know as self-hypnosis, begin with a syllogism. This time it goes as follows:

"For contentment within myself, such positive attitudes as cheerfulness, optimism and enthusiasm are essential.

"I need contentment within myself in order to live comfortably.

"To the degree that I wish to live comfortably, I'll allow myself to experience the dominant feelings of cheerfulness, optimism and enthusiasm."

Once the syllogism is pronounced, we move as usual to the imagery. Here you are alone. The purpose is to encourage you to let yourself feel happily content when not in communication with other people, to allow yourself to move through the fun and fury of daily life in a dominant mood of good cheer. People around you may be gnashing their teeth and furrowing their brows while you, in your visualizing, see yourself observing them and their teapot tempests with good humor, and remarking, "Well, that's their problem." By contrast, you assert your freedom to feel cheerful and optimistic despite all. You may see yourself passing a newsstand, where a headline proclaims, "WORLD COMES TO END!" So? You look up at the sky and see that it's bright and blue, whereupon you shrug your shoulders, smile and say, "*Let* the world come to an end; that's its problem. Personally, I think it's a lovely day."

Of course this has a Pollyanna ring. But it's all right to swing to one extreme in order to achieve a healthy balance somewhere in the middle. So envision yourself smiling through the miseries of other people and even through your own: see yourself going to your mailbox, taking out a letter, opening it and reading, "We are sorry to report. . . ." And you say, "So what? I can take that. I've had worse news than this and survived." You see yourself put the letter into your pocket and whistle your way back into the house.

Envision yourself withstanding the contusions and abrasions of life as if you were protected by an invisible plastic shell. You declare your constitutional right to the pursuit of your own happiness. You may imagine yourself (literally) walking through rain and snow, hail and sleet—even, to mangle the metaphor, through fire and brimstone—and the more it pours, the more you smile. You're happy and content. You're immune: nothing can touch you; nothing can get through your shield of cheerfulness. You allow yourself to feel buoyantly optimistic and enthusiastic, no matter what the twistings and turnings of world events or personal fortune. You are hopelessly, irredeemably cheerful.

Following your visualizing, give yourself the posthypnotic suggestion that the positive image you see on the wall will stick in your mind and that you will float smilingly through the rest of the day, impervious to the negatives that bog other people down and that used to bog you down. You see through them, you see above them and you see beyond them. With such projections into the future, you close your session with yourself and emerge from the relaxed state feeling quite refreshed, cheerful and alive.

Tact

It turns out that we make our planetary sojourn easier on ourselves if we couch the truth in tactful words. To be sure, being truthful while considering the feelings of others is a difficult and delicate balance to achieve, but why should you not develop it? Self-hypnosis can come to your aid if you find yourself inadvertently blurting out truths that have you muttering later, "I could have bitten my tongue off!" To spare yourself such self-mutilation, allow yourself a syllogism instead:

"For favorable relations with others, to be tactless is ruinous.

"I need favorable relations with others in order to live comfortably.

"Therefore, to the degree that I want to live comfortably, I'll allow myself to handle facts and opinions in a tactful way."

From there we move to the visualizing. Maybe you're the type who sees a friend who looks awful today and says to him, "Gee, you look awful today." Truth: 100; Tact: 0. You need to strike a balance between the two. See yourself, then, greeting him with a warm smile, thereby telling the truth about your friendly feelings. Visualize yourself uttering a strong welcome. He opens up and explains his sad look, giving you an opportunity to strengthen your friendship with a little sympathy and understanding.

Or your wife or girl friend may ask you whether she should wear her polka-dot dress out to dinner tonight. That's a touchy one. You don't want to lie about it, but you don't like the dress very much. You envision yourself replying diplomatically, "You always look great to me, but you know how much I like you in the blue and white stripes," or in similar words suitable to your own style. Not the *whole* truth, perhaps, but still the truth, and you have avoided being needlessly unkind.

You then engage in the customary posthypnotic suggestion, telling yourself that you will avoid kicking people in the shins verbally in the name of truth-telling. On the other hand, you will abstain from telling some blatant lie on the grounds that you're being tactful. Rather, you will hew to the truth, but the truth that you tell won't injure others and won't hurt you, because it's tempered with tact.

Poise and Courage

Poise and courage are close relatives. To maintain poise, for instance, when a fire alarm sounds is also to show courage. This doesn't mean that you prove your courage by standing still and watching the fire burn you up—courage is not the same as stupidity. What it means is that you make the moves that will serve to your advantage: to summon help, to put out the fire yourself or to flee.

As another example, you display courage when, in the presence of unfriendly people or in a hostile situation, you remain calm and self-contained rather than trembling and stammering or breaking out in a cold sweat.

What are some situations that might call for the exercise of poise and courage? A young man pays a visit to the parents of his girl friend when he knows they disapprove of him. A representative of management enters a union meeting with an offer he has been directed to make but which he knows will be angrily rejected. A doctoral candidate appears before the committee to take his oral exams. A political candidate makes a statement of concession. It's any situation, in short, from which you would much prefer to slink silently away.

Instead, try the self-hypnotic exercise, beginning with the mental recitation of a syllogism, such as:

"For favorable feelings within myself and for effective relations with others, an attitude of courage and poise is essential.

"I need these favorable relations with myself and with others in order to live comfortably.

"To the degree that I want to live comfortably, I'll allow myself to feel and extend a courageous poise."

The imagery speaks for itself. On that magical movie screen in your mind, conjure up the scene that most demands the poise and courage you need in order for you to function as you would like. If an actor, a public speaker or a minister, you will see yourself before your group, large or small, feeling that ease which bespeaks inner poise and a state of strength and courage. You observe yourself standing tall, smiling, self-confident and articulate. When you finish, the people in your audience nod their approval to each other, applaud you enthusiastically, even cheer.

I have a salesman patient from whom I received a postcard one day with just two words, in capital letters: "IT WORKED!" He had known for more than a week beforehand of a meeting at which salesmen would be video-taped as they engaged in mock sales. That is, his superior would sit opposite him at a table while the camera and the tape were rolling and would say, "So you want to sell me half a million clocks, do ya? Why should I buy them from you?"

My patient understandably wanted to feel at ease in this situation, so, starting ten days before the event, several times a day and before going to sleep at night, he would induce the relaxed state of self-hypnosis. Then he did three things:

(1) During the silent recitation of the syllogism, he asserted that the usual nervousness and tightening up that he had theretofore experienced would be a poison to his professional life.

(2) He pictured himself rising and shaking the customer's hand as the man thanked him for selling him the articles, then moving off the platform, and the fellow salesmen who had been watching the video tape congratulating him.

(3) Through posthypnotic affirmations, he foresaw that he would find himself thoroughly comfortable and relaxed at the meeting, and that it would be a rewarding, exhilarating and expansive experience for him and for his customer (or, in this case, for his superior, playing the role of customer).

To his mild surprise but immense delight, he found that his fantasized scenario came to be played out in the actual sales meeting.

The same approach would apply in a one-to-one situation, perhaps with an individual with whom you have previously had poor relations. You see yourself on the screen now, meeting that person and transmitting signals of your new-found poise and courage. You observe his expression of surprise over your mastery of the situation, as well as a look of pleasure and self-satisfaction on your own face.

There will likewise be incidents requiring the exercise of poise and courage that don't relate to people at all, but that involve things, such as bad news in a letter or on the television screen or radio. Or it may be an event that would seem inconsequential to others but has you cringing—a thunderstorm on a dark night, perhaps. You see it happening on the screen: a bolt of lightning and a sharp clap of thunder. You observe yourself watching and listening as the storm rages around you, but you remain undisturbed and unaffected, strong and cool, in full control of all your faculties.

You then give yourself a posthypnotic suggestion to that point: that whatever the stressful event—a confrontation with unfriendly people or a distressing situation—you will find that your response will be one of calm and comfort, of poise and courage, sharply distinct from any previous less positive reactions.

And then you emerge from the raised state.

Ambition

Many people go through life in neutral, wishing that they had more ambition. They see others surge ahead, and they say to themselves, "No wonder: he's more motivated than I am." Or they attribute others' good fortune to luck or "the breaks," never acknowledging that for the most part successful people engineer their own breaks. Individuals of little initiative exist in a state of suspended action, waiting for something to happen *to them* rather than the reverse. A man will say, "I'd like to be a more successful salesman, but . . ." or "I'm tired of being a clerical lawyer. I'd like to be in the courtroom, dramatically presenting my case, but I don't know; I just . . ." What such people need is a dose of get-up-and-go to enable them to move to their own advantage.

Psychologists have long wrestled with this problem: how do you put a fire under someone who is unmotivated? It's a dilemma with few satisfactory solutions, but you can guess one possibility. Self-hypnosis, during which you picture yourself as possessing that motivation you do not at the moment feel, will gradually build it. You'll just have to take that statement on faith until you try the system. But I invite you to try this method several times a day for as little as two or three weeks. I challenge you, at the end of this trial period of diligent practice, to write me and say that you remain the jellyfish you were before. Something will happen to you, or else the experiences I have had in my consulting room are exceptions—which is possible, but not likely. Give it a chance.

First, put yourself in the raised state, then provide yourself with a syllogism, such as:

"For my self-respect and my feelings of self-worth, lack of

motivation, an attitude of helpless let-come-what-may, is a poison.

"I need my self-respect and feelings of self-worth in order to live in comfort.

"To the degree that I want to live comfortably, I'll allow myself to feel increasingly ambitious."

This, of course, just begs for a certain kind of imagery. You see yourself, on that familiar movie screen, with a straighter spine, a firmer chin, an eye more steely and a general demeanor of self-assurance and full-throttle ambition. You know where you're going and how to get there. Envision yourself not just sitting idly by, wishing you had a certain job or position, but assertively moving forward and taking the steps that will lead you to your goal.

Let's say you are now a secretary and would like to be editor of some magazine. Imagine yourself moving up, a stage at a time, from secretary to editorial assistant to associate editor to senior editor and into the managing editor's chair itself. Every move is made with confidence as you master the skills and knowledge required at each level.

Instead of being on the assembly line, would you like to be the foreman? Name it in the syllogism—that for the increase of your income and self-satisfaction, to remain at your present level is ruinous—and picture your progress happening on the screen.

If you're an elevator operator and you want to rise in the world beyond the highest floor the elevator can take you to, picture it. See yourself being called into the office of the building manager and offered the position of superintendent. You thank him, return to your home and spread the word to your family and friends, who congratulate you enthusiastically.

Picture yourself as the ambitious achiever you notice other people are and wish you yourself were. Watch it happening. Observe yourself on the screen, a step ahead of others on your way to the top. You may imagine climbing an actual ladder, on the uppermost rung of which is a sign with the title of the position you want and the inscription, "Reserved for [your name]." You can make it happen.

You may say, "But I don't have any career interests; that's my trouble." You don't want to be editor of a magazine or chief justice of the appellate court or the top salesman in your company. You tell me that you don't know what you want to be when you grow up (even though you've already reached your majority). No problem. Simply picture yourself as knowing what you want: the you on the screen knows something the flesh-and-blood you doesn't know yet, that's all. So picture that person on the screen (yourself) as having decided what you want and now moving ahead with firm and determined step to achieve it.

Finally, give yourself a posthypnotic suggestion: "When I emerge from this state, I'll find myself gradually firming up a single purpose and confidently and eagerly taking the steps that will lead me to it."

And you begin doing just that as you emerge from the relaxed state.

CHAPTER 11

Sharpening Skills of Mind and Body

The professional athlete gets even better, while the amateur stops being the butt of tennis-court jokes.

The bridge, chess or tiddlywinks player begins to win more games than he loses.

The secretary types more swiftly and accurately and takes faster dictation.

The salesman sells more; the carpenter cuts straighter; the executive manages better.

The singer sings sweetly; the writer writes vividly; the painter paints beautifully.

Students learn more while studying less.

On goes the list; the possibilities are manifold. Self-hypnosis, indeed, can help you hone your skills, enhance your performance and increase your efficiency in virtually any endeavor you undertake: at work, at play or for general self-improvement. There *is* one catch, but it's far from a Catch-22. It's a catch that it is safe to say most people can handle: it's simply that you must have the *capacity* to function at a higher level, the potential to be better. Self-hypnosis will not magically implant talent and ability where none exists—it won't make you a concert pianist if you're tone deaf or a running back if you trip tying your own shoes. What it will do is help you to capitalize on your strong points and strengthen your performance in areas where your interests and aptitudes lie. Remember "accentuate the positive"?

So, if you have a desire to polish a specific skill—athletic, creative, business, mechanical, study, recreational—to increase efficiency in *any* activity or, through a fascinating trick known as time distortion, either to expand or compress the time you have, this chapter offers the wherewithal.

To begin, let's look at sports.

Athletic

On February 5, 1977, *The New York Times* carried a story under this two-column headline: "Hypnosis Helps Tickner Realize Skating Dream." Charlie Tickner had just won the United States men's figure-skating championship with an electrifying display on the ice that earned him three "perfect" scores and a standing ovation. The story related that in previous competitions Tickner's lack of self-confidence had prevented him from giving the performance he was physically and artistically capable of delivering. So, a few months previously, on the advice of his coach, he had turned to self-hypnosis "to build up self-confidence, my energy, my relaxation." In addition, he began to visually "run through" his routine before skating it, thus combining the elements of the relaxed state and the visualization we've been offering in this book. The rest, as they say, is history.

Psychology Today (July 1976) reported on a similar technique in an article called "Body Thinking: Psychology for Olympic Champs." In his article, Dr. Richard M. Suinn described his work with champion athletes: "I call my method 'visuo-motor behavior rehearsal,' or VMBR. The method can be divided simply into relaxation . . . and the use of imagery for strengthening psychological or motor skills."

Though called VMBR, the procedure incorporates the same aim and techniques as the self-hypnosis practiced by ice-skater Tickner. A similar, less formal approach was taken by the 1976 U.S. Olympic men's swimming coach, Dr. James Counsilman, who had his swimmers relax and then visualize in their minds the races they would be swimming. The team brought home an unprecedented twelve gold medals.

Whatever you call it, the practice of putting yourself into a relaxed state, followed by a mental visual rehearsal of how you wish to perform a given action can, without question, aid you immeasurably in actually doing so.

The athlete who psychs himself up before the competition and the coach who inspires his team with an incendiary pep talk to perform as they've never performed before are both reinforcing the suggestion that the athlete is capable of delivering more, that he has an untapped potential. Though neither coach nor competitor is consciously practicing hypnosis, there is strong suspicion in some quarters (including this one) that the athlete spontaneously experiences an altered state of consciousness which permits him to exceed his previous performance.

It is often when playing under pressure that one most needs the cool serenity that self-hypnosis provides. Many people have had the experience of performing smoothly and skillfully during practice or while playing strictly for pleasure, but of "clutching" in actual competition. As Peter Blythe writes in *Hypnotism: Its Power and Practice:*

"All this tension in golf and other personal competitive games can be diminished or eliminated by hypnotic suggestion. . . . Lawrie Fouchee took twenty-three putts to cover nine holes, and that was about his average. He was then placed in the hypnotic trance and told . . . that he would play a more relaxed and accurate round. Immediately afterwards he played the same nine holes again, and this time he was able to sink them in a startling seventeen putts."

Blythe points out that hypnosis does not give the golfer more skill; it just allows the individual to play to the best of his ability. There is no reason you should not be able to do exactly the same thing, whether you are whacking the ball around for pleasure or playing at the Masters for fame and money. Amateur or professional, you can use self-hypnosis to enhance both pleasure and performance. This goes for all athletic skills, whether swimming, tennis, golf, football, baseball, basketball, wrestling, boxing, bowling, track, table tennis—you name it.

As for procedure, simply choose the sport in which you want to better your performance and make the appropriate modifications in the three sections that make up the self-hypnosis: syllogism, imagery, and posthypnotic suggestion. Let us choose tennis for illustrative purposes here. If your interest is in rope skipping or any sport other than tennis, use your ingenuity to fashion the words of the syllogism and posthypnotic suggestion, as well as the content of the imagery, to conform to your chosen sport.

In devising your syllogism, you should first consider the purpose of your game. That is, if you come to tennis for the improvement of your health—if your doctor has said to you, "I would suggest that you keep your muscles in tone by playing tennis"—that objective will dictate the terms of the syllogism. Here is one possibility:

"For my bodily health, not for me but for my bodily health, abstaining from physical exercise is a kind of poison.

"I need my bodily health in order to live.

"Therefore, to the degree that I want to live, I will engage in a regular tennis program."

On the other hand, if you're playing at Wimbledon next week against Jimmy Connors, your aim will be not to improve your health at the moment, but to win, and you will compose a syllogism accordingly. For example:

"For my self-regard as well as for the regard of my teammates and the club and/or country that I represent, to play a losing game of tennis is a kind of poison.

"I need my own self-regard and that of my teammates and spectators in order to live to the fullest.

"To the degree that I want to live to the fullest, I will play a winning, triumphant tennis match."

Most people will fall somewhere between these two extremes—of just exercising in a sport in order to improve their health or of representing their country in an international match. We want to play croquet because it's fun, but some of us also like to win. Be creative and design your syllogism to suit your own aims.

Following the syllogism, you imagine the movie screen on which you will project pictures of yourself in the game, accomplishing your objective. If your purpose is simply to exercise your body so that you'll be a healthy specimen, then watch yourself playing tennis with a friend, having fun on a pleasant afternoon. You see the ball sail over the net; you move into position and send it back; your strokes are easy and accurate. You move about the court with the grace of an accomplished athlete, achieving your goal of exercise and fun. You watch yourself enjoying the game.

But if your goal is to win the match for yourself, the team or the United States, then this time, as you watch yourself on the screen, you'll shift the emphasis to winning.

See yourself ready to serve. Bounce the ball and look over the net, taking the measure of the court and of your opponent. You know that the first ball is going in. Ball in the air, racquet, over the net easily, out of reach of your opponent. It's an ace. Move to the other side of the court, feeling comfortable and reasonably sure that you will perform the ace again. The same smooth serve. If he hits the ball back, you find yourself moving gracefully into position and stroking the ball with accuracy and speed. It drops into his court out of reach again, and you've won a second point.

Continue this: watching the ball, watching your racquet, watching your opponent, watching the net and the court. You feel in a state of ease and confidence as you move rapidly about the court, alert, effective, always in charge. You see yourself walk to the net at the close of the match, shake your opponent's hand and smilingly acknowledge the applause of the onlookers. You can even imagine a headline on the front page of the next day's newspaper: "——— Sweeps Tennis Finals: 6–0, 6–0, 6–0," along with a photograph of you as the victor. Only your imagination sets a limit on where you can carry this visualization.

Finally, the posthypnotic suggestion is directed to the same point: "When I emerge from this state I will find myself in an airy, almost floating state, calm and comfortable, very much in charge of myself and confident that I will win tomorrow's match." Or, if the objective is simply to get yourself onto the tennis court in order to exercise, you will head right for the tennis court and look on it with interest and eagerness. If your problem is that, once on the court, you don't enjoy playing, even though you want to, then that is your posthypnotic suggestion: this afternoon's (or tomorrow's) game will be an enjoyable one; it will seem somehow light and fun and easy, more so than it's ever appeared before. Picture the positive and talk to yourself in positive terms in this posthypnotic suggestion. And then, of course, emerge in the usual way.

You should engage in self-hypnosis several days before any big match, meet or game and every couple of hours on the day itself. Your self-hypnosis will have the following results: the closer the starting time draws, the more calm, comfortable and confident you will become, your muscles relaxed yet alert, and your interest in the coming contest keen. Furthermore, you will be encouraging and inspiring to your teammates.

Mechanical

You may want to apply to more practical pursuits the same types of physical skills and adroitness required in athletics. Are you a home repairman who wishes he were handier? Are you a secretary who's all thumbs when it comes to making adjustments on office machinery? Perhaps you want to go to the top of your craft—carpentry, masonry, plumbing—or to graduate from truck driver to crane operator. Or you may be a tailor, barber or repairman who simply wants to get better at that profession.

In any case, you will want to build your syllogism around your particular line of work or interest. For example, let's consider the automobile repairman:

"For my increased income as well as my self-esteem, a slow and fumbling use of tools is ruinous.

"I need an increased income and self-esteem in order to live well.

"To the degree that I want to live well, I will handle my tools with the highest degree of dexterity."

Now to the imagery. There is the car engine, on your wall movie screen, and here are your tools. As you begin to work on the engine you notice that the proper tool fairly leaps into your hand. You use it swiftly and expertly, lay it down; the next needed tool jumps into your hand; you finish the next task, and so on until the job is completed swiftly, smoothly and skillfully.

As a posthypnotic suggestion you say to yourself, "When I leave this chair, I'll experience greater confidence and greater skill in applying my tools than I have known before, skill that will grow day after day."

And you emerge from the raised state.

If you are not trying to increase your skills for financial or professional reasons, but just for their own sake, simply leave out that part of the syllogism referring to "increased income" and substitute "For my comfort [as well as my self-esteem]."

Mental

What mental skills would you like to sharpen? Do you want to improve your concentration, to comprehend better, to remember more? Would you like to read faster or study more efficiently? Add a column of figures more swiftly and accurately? Might your bridge or chess game be better? It's yours for the asking.

We'll divide the mental skills into four subcategories—concentration, comprehension, memory and games—and discuss each in turn.

CONCENTRATION

Concentration is a quality of mind useful to all. The house painter concentrates carefully lest he spill his paint or fall off his ladder. The storekeeper concentrates so that his records will accurately reflect the exchange of goods for money. The cabdriver holds his mind firmly to his task in order to retain control of the car and follow the best route to his destination. The student concentrates hard in order to absorb his study material and perform well in examinations.

Or consider an actress, a patient of mine, who reported that when she came onstage her mind wandered to the scenery, or to her shoes, and she began wondering who was in the audience. Consequently, she forgot her lines and broke character, lapses that were proving to be highly detrimental to her career. By way of self-hypnotic therapy to correct her problem, she was advised to begin with the following syllogism:

"For my self-esteem and the esteem of my fellow actors and the audience, mind-wandering is poisonous.

"I need the esteem of myself and others in order to succeed in my profession.

"To the degree that I want to succeed in my profession, I'll engage in sharpest concentration."

Second, imagery: there's the stage in your mind's eye. You enter, find that your lines come readily and that you stay in character. You play out the scene, performing at your best. When you finish you see that the audience applauds you enthusiastically as you smilingly and graciously bow.

As a posthypnotic suggestion, tell yourself that onstage you'll find your mind to be exclusively confined to the character you're playing and completely absorbed in the lines of the play.

Or suppose you are a student accustomed to being easily distracted by friendly interruptions, blasting radios, trains passing by, etc. Devise yourself such a syllogism as:

"To earn promotion and graduation, allowing distraction from my studies is a poison.

"I need promotion and graduation in order to achieve my life goals.

"To the degree that I want to achieve my life goals, I'll give unrelenting attention to the study material at hand."

On to visualization. Maybe you're sitting not at a desk but outside under a leafy oak tree on a fine spring afternoon. You watch yourself on the screen, stretched out, warm and comfortable. The sun is shining, people are strolling by, birds are chirping, and you find it easy and enjoyable to concentrate on your studies. You absorb without strain the written material, in the midst of whatever might have previously distracted you. Trucks roll by, children toss a ball past your head and jackhammers scream, but nothing can disturb you now. You are entranced by your reading. Feel free to change the setting. Any modification you make in the imagery will be important, because such changes make it yours.

Then comes the posthypnotic suggestion. Since an essential characteristic of hypnosis itself is heightened concentration, if you sometimes have trouble concentrating on your studies, it should prove helpful to give yourself the instruction that upon emerging from the raised state you will find that your ability to concentrate will be comparable to that which you experience while practicing self-hypnosis. Your interest in the subject at hand will be so keen and your determination to complete it so strong that any distraction that might interfere with your doing so will be shut out of your awareness.

Finally, of course, you emerge from the relaxed state.

COMPREHENSION

The person interested in increasing his comprehension may range from the grade-school student uncertain of his life's direction all the way up to the country's Chief Executive, who has achieved his final work objective. If, as we understand, President Carter has taken a course to increase his reading speed and comprehension, you too might find that improving your own comprehension of material read or heard is a valuable asset.

Do you attend business meetings and find that you fail to follow the main line of discussion? Are you a student whose lagging comprehension of your subjects has lowered your grades? Or do you wish to comprehend more just for your own enjoyment and self-satisfaction? Whatever the circumstances that have you in need of heightened understanding, self-hypnosis can be of use.

Suppose you are an executive accustomed to attending meetings where the discussion grows loose and discursive and the main issue gets lost in a morass of minor points. You want to be the one who sees through the verbal fog to the real issues. First, the syllogism:

"For the effectiveness of my business meetings, letting main issues get lost among minor ones is destructive.

"I need effective business meetings in order to achieve personal and company success.

"To the degree that I want personal and company success, my mind will ably grasp essentials."

For the imagery part of his self-hypnosis the executive pictures a representative meeting. He sees himself, on his imaginary movie screen, listening eagerly to the discussion, seizing on the vital point and rising to clarify and explain it to his colleagues. His comprehension of the complex subject meets with grateful approval from his colleagues, and he smilingly receives their thanks and congratulations.

As a posthypnotic suggestion he tells himself, "At my next gathering with my fellow executives it will be my pleasure to pinpoint, swiftly and accurately, the salient aspects of any issue under discussion."

Just how helpful hypnosis can be as an aid to improving comprehension in studies was demonstrated in an experiment at Monterey Peninsula College in California, reported by Dr. Peter Mutke in *The American Journal of Clinical Hypnosis* (April 1967). In the experiment, one group of students was taught the Dan-Ro System of Remedial Reading while under hypnosis, and a second group learned the same method without hypnosis. After five or six sessions the hypnotized students reached a reading comprehension of 78 percent, a level it took the unhypnotized students twenty-two sessions to achieve.

In another fascinating experiment at the Child Center in Kentfield, California,* a group of eight- to twelve-year-olds were taught how to induce self-hypnosis in themselves. While in this state, each child was instructed to imagine himself lifting his brain out of his head, placing it on the ground and using a garden hose to wash out all of the old ideas that interfere with learning. Then he was told to see himself on a movie screen, reading fluently and without effort—reading with pleasure.

The child was next told to walk up onto the screen and right into his own body. Finally, the suggestion was made that this pleasant picture was passing into his blood cells, up through his blood vessels and fusing with every part of his body. He was becoming, then, that person who reads so successfully and happily. It was further suggested that each person would see and feel this picture at various times throughout the day and night. The group was told to practice the autosuggestion (read "self-hypnosis") technique for five minutes once or twice daily.

Two months later, the children following this technique were tested and their performance was compared with that of a control group made up of children who had similar reading problems but who had not engaged in self-hypnosis. Speed, accuracy and comprehension increased an average of 1.6 years for the experimental group, but only 4 months for the control group. In addition, the self-esteem of the experimentals, that is, how they felt about themselves, increased at twice the rate of that of the control group.

It may be that you just want to increase comprehension of what you read for your own enjoyment and self-satisfaction. If so, you'll find it to your advantage to revise the syllogism and

* Gerald G. Jampolsky, M.D., and Gayl Westerman, M.S., *A Unique Suggestive and Auto Suggestive Technique to Help Children with Reading Problems* (Kentfield, California: The Child Center, 1973).

imagery accordingly, then try such posthypnotic implants as:
"When I now read a book I will begin by taking it in first in
words, next week in sentences, then in paragraphs and ideas.
It will be easier and easier for me to get at the kernel of
meaning in what I read and hear. I'll do so more accurately
than people spending much more time at it; my level of
comprehension will be far above the average."

And then you emerge from the raised state.

MEMORY

Perhaps while writing you can't call up a needed word.
Telephone numbers slip away. Maybe you encounter what's-
his-name on the street and feel embarrassed when you stop to
chat. If only you could recall that hazy past event with clarity.
Daily life is packed with people and occurrences, many of
which are best forgotten, but some of which you desperately
want to remember. Self-hypnosis can furnish the means of
doing so. Begin with a syllogism along these lines:

"For my personal and professional benefit, lapses in memory are disastrous.

"I need personal and professional benefit in order to live in
comfort.

"To the degree that I want to live in comfort, I'll allow myself
to remember what I want to remember."

For imagery, suppose you're a door-to-door salesperson.
See yourself, on the white screen, meeting a former customer
on the street, clearly recalling her face and name and the
articles she favors. You greet her, calling her by name, and ask
her whether she needs some more of the items she has previously bought. You visualize her answering that she does, and
you arrange a time of delivery to her home.

If a student, cast your syllogism in words appropriate to
your situation, then visualize. You see yourself opening a book
and devouring the material as if it were as enjoyable as sitting
down to a steak done exactly to your taste. Your mind is active;
your eyes are bright. You flip the pages, and all the facts, all the
figures, all the details leave the book and file themselves away

in the computer of your mind, ready to be called forth whenever you want them. Your mind is just brimming with information. Finally, you see yourself rising with a smile of self-satisfaction and in a state of triumph.

Before emerging from the relaxed state, give yourself post-hypnotic suggestions along whatever lines of memory you want to improve, such as:

"I'll find that, increasingly, the information which it's helpful for me to recall will come to me. The needed word will appear, the lost telephone number will pop into my head, the elusive name will come to mind, the fuzzy past event will materialize clearly. Memory will become one of the attributes I pride myself on and that people compliment me on. It will be easier to recall facts, figures, events, feelings and thoughts, whether in conversation, my own reflection, my work or my studies. The whole process will be effortless."

GAMES

By improving such skills as concentration, comprehension and memory, you may also develop the mental dexterity required in such games as bridge, poker or chess. Let's say it's chess you're interested in. You first compose yourself a syllogism, such as:

"For my self-satisfaction, to play a lackluster game of chess is harmful.

"I need my self-satisfaction to live at peace with myself.

"To the degree that I wish to live at peace with myself, I'll play chess with imagination and inspiration."

Then the imagery. You see the chess board in front of you on your imaginary screen. Opening moves suddenly loom as having new possibilities, and you watch the game progress, your every move a shrewd and effective one. You marshal your forces, seek out your opponent's knights and ultimately trap his king.

You reinforce such imagery with a posthypnotic suggestion that the next time you play chess you will see the board from a greater distance, yet with sharper clarity. A series of moves will occur to you that will permit you to home in on the opposition, especially on the king and queen, and you will find yourself winning the game almost automatically.

And then you emerge from the relaxed state.

Efficiency and Organizational Ability

Can you organize your time efficiently and perform the tasks of your daily life in a disciplined way? Or do magazines and newspapers pile up unread on the promise of the morrow? Are your bills paid on time, or do you receive dunning notices reminding you of your delinquency? Do letters go unanswered? Perhaps your bank informs you that your account is overdrawn, and you wonder, "How did that ever happen?"

Whatever aspect of efficiency you wish to increase, wherever you want to channel your energy, in whatever way you'd like to discipline yourself further, you can do it through the therapy of self-hypnosis. It's a well-documented finding that by lowering tension and raising concentration, this method can elevate a person's efficiency. To do so, start with a syllogism:

"For practical daily management, inefficiency and lack of organization are damaging.

"I need my day to be well managed in order for me to live comfortably.

"To the degree that I want to live comfortably, I'll organize matters efficiently."

For imagery, let's suppose that you are one of the host of humans who could use some sharpening of their use of time in starting their day. Watch the screen. The alarm rings. You see yourself rise from the bed, step into the shower and perform your ablutions swiftly. You don your clothes with rapid ease. Your breakfast is before you, and you consume it in expeditious comfort. Coat on, you're out the door in plenty of time to catch the 8:06 express. Throughout this routine you have been relaxed and smiling—it's a pleasure.

Before emerging from your self-hypnosis you give yourself

a posthypnotic suggestion: tomorrow morning, upon awakening, I'll move through the procedure of starting the day with a pleasing new efficiency.

Choose the area in which you wish to become more efficient and create a syllogism and imagery to fit it, following which, before emerging from the raised state, you will give yourself a posthypnotic suggestion. Let's assume you want to enhance your efficiency on the job. Here is a sample implant:

"I will go to my desk and dispose of whatever is there in order of importance. If the phone rings, I will suggest that I return the call later, unless it's of greater importance. If a co-worker drops in to chat, I will politely but firmly suggest that we talk at a later time. I will stay at my desk until I've completed the tasks I've set myself."

Some other suggestions:

Secretary: "My fingers will race over the typewriter, hitting the keys with a speed and accuracy greater than I've known before, and the rate will become habitual. I'll be finished with the material well before the time it's needed. The entire office will be a cheerful environment and my work a pleasant experience."

Factory worker: "Any dissatisfaction or boredom I feel on the assembly line will be translated into increased efficiency. I'll either be so pleased with my improved performance and new attitude that I'll want to stay where I am, or I'll perform so well that I'll be promoted to something higher."

Executive: "I'll feel totally relaxed at the conference table, in control of myself and the situation. As my eyes sweep the entire group, my colleagues will feel magnetized. The meeting will go swiftly and smoothly as I achieve all of the objectives I've set."

Work Performance

Actually, there can be no sharp delineation of work skills as such, for whatever the job, be it surgery or sweeping, various skills dovetail and overlap to make up a profession. For example, a secretary surely uses a variety of mental and mechanical skills, as well as rather more personal ones as she deals with her boss, peers, visitors and telephone callers. So the range of skills required to succeed in the work world can be broad.

Fortunately, we don't have to consider them individually, for whatever the heading we put them under, the method for improving them remains the same (although the details of verbal and visual implants vary, depending on the nature of the job). To narrow down to one, we'll choose selling as an example. Let a mediocre salesman turn himself into a top-notch performer. He can aim at becoming the best salesman in his company, or maybe it's just his own record he wants to better, to sell $2,000 worth of merchandise this week instead of his customary $1,000 worth. Techniques are available for him to do either. First, the syllogism:

"For the enlargement of both my self-satisfaction and my income, a static sales record is self-damaging.

"I need my self-satisfaction and income in order to live comfortably.

"To the degree that I want to live comfortably, I'll maximize my selling skills."

If you've followed the self-improvement techniques up to now, it's clear what the salesman will picture. The procedure may be automatic, but there must be nothing automatic about your imagery: it must be vibrantly alive. On that imaginary wall screen you, the salesman, see yourself entering the office of the merchandise manager with whom you have an appointment. There's an aura of success, of self-assurance and of likability about you that he can't resist. You watch him listening to you spellbound. You're fluid; you're lucid; you present your material in an irresistible way. You see him nodding in agreement, thanking you, shaking your hand and—signing that $100,000 order. You leave, beaming with satisfaction, knowing that you have accomplished your objective.

You can carry the image wherever you want. You may go home to your partner and see her throw her arms around you. You may tell your fellow salesmen and your superior about it and enjoy their congratulations. You see it all on the screen as they shake your hand and clap you on the back. You might even dance about—this is your show. There's nothing silly about cheering yourself on. What you see on the screen is transformed into the lifeblood of success in whatever you wish to achieve.

Then give yourself a posthypnotic suggestion: "Following my emergence from this state I will feel a new surge of confidence. My manner will be relaxed and self-assured, and the words will flow smoothly. The people I contact will receive me with open arms and open pocketbooks."

Then you emerge from the relaxed state.

This example can, of course, be adapted to any work situation where you want to better your performance—whether you're a service worker trying to increase your tips or a vice-president trying to increase profits.

Creativity

Rachmaninoff composed his famous Second Piano Concerto while undergoing hypnotherapy to help him out of his depression over the unfavorable reception of his previous composition. So appreciative was he for what hypnosis had done that he dedicated this concerto to his hypnotherapist.

Hypnosis—and *self*-hypnosis—can help to enhance a host of creative skills. Is it your musical composition or performance that you want to improve? Are you a painter, an illustrator, a sculptor? Are you a photographer who wants to perfect your craft? Are you a journalist, a novelist, a poet, a playwright?

Offered here is a method of doing with your skill that which you most want to do. If you're a writer, for example, do you wish to write gracefully just to enjoy reading your own material? Or do you want to be recognized as a serious novelist, an expert at nonfiction, a writer of comedy material? Your choice will influence the words you say to yourself and the pictures you see during your self-hypnosis. As a model, let us try this syllogism:

"For my self-satisfaction and for others' approval, to per-form at a level below my maximum is self-damaging.

"I need my self-satisfaction and the approval of others in order to live comfortably.

"To the degree that I wish to live comfortably, I'll perform to the utmost limits of my ability."

Whatever your particular interest might be, your imagination and creativity are vital, and you can exercise them both in forming your imagery. On your imaginary screen you see yourself sitting down at your easel if you're about to paint, approaching your desk if it's writing you're engaged in, as-suming your seat at the piano if you're a pianist, etc. You watch yourself approach your working materials enthusiastically, with ideas racing through your head. As you observe yourself, you see that you pick up your pencil or brush with assurance and that your ideas flow effortlessly through them and onto the paper or canvas until your project is completed. You smile; you're happy and satisfied with what you have created. You can exaggerate the scene just as much as you wish. Your feeling of triumph can be so intense that you jump up and down and clap your hands like a child. You might even reward yourself with a special treat. There is just no limit here to the delight you allow yourself to take in performing well at your art.

You want then to fertilize your imagery with a posthypnotic suggestion that upon emerging from this state you will feel in full possession and control of your usual sensations, added to which there will be a new confidence, a new feeling of ease and pleasant floating that propels you in the direction of your materials. When you sit down at your desk, take up your instrument or pick up the paintbrush, it will be with a fresh sense of confidence and renewed interest and enthusiasm in the project.

If a pianist, you can tell yourself that your fingers will be so supple and quick that they will seem to fly over the keyboard; the music will jump right from your fingers without your thinking about it. If an artist, you suggest that your imagina-tion will be at its height, your colors will be vivid and true, the work will be emotionally evocative, etc. All of this will be accompanied by the knowledge that you have the ability to accomplish your work in such a way that it will be a delight both to you and to your listeners if it is music, to your readers if it is writing or to your viewers if it is a visual art.

Then, of course, the customary three-two-one procedure of emergence from the raised state.

Time Distortion

Are there occasions in your life when you say, "I can't wait until . . ." either for a pleasant event to start or for a trying one, such as time in the dentist's chair, to end?

Conversely, do you ever feel squeezed for time and wish that you had more—to prepare for an exam, for instance?

Each represents an occasion when you would like to distort time, in the first case to compress it and in the second to expand it. Both are possible with self-hypnosis.

Let us take up time compression first. Patients have told me that when they use the threefold self-therapy of syllogism, imagery and posthypnotic suggestion, the time it takes a dentist to extract or fill a tooth seems to fly by. Now, that's remarkable! Let's take the dental experience as our model of time compression. First, the syllogism:

"For my bodily health and comfort, to perceive this dental-chair experience as a lengthy one is a kind of poison.

"I need my bodily health and comfort in order to live in contentment.

"To the degree that I wish to live in contentment, I'll mentally compress the dental-chair time."

Then comes the visualization, wherein you see yourself on the screen in the dentist's office. You sit down in the dental chair; the dentist works on your tooth; he's finished; you get up. By its very nature this has to be a brief visualization, almost like an early movie, in which all movement speeds up. But you can keep rerunning the film. You go back into the dentist's office and sit in the chair; he bends down; he says, "We're finished"; you get up and leave. You may repeat the sequence any number of times.

You follow with a posthypnotic suggestion that the dental experience will seem like a matter of seconds or at most minutes of painless happenings. (If you wish to reduce the pain itself during dental treatment, consult the earlier section on pain.) You can tell yourself that the expected half-hour in the dentist's chair will pass in three minutes.

You then emerge from the raised state. As a practical matter, I would suggest engaging in such an exercise several times a day for two or three days before the visit, then again just before leaving for the appointment, and finally in the dentist's office itself.

Now, the other side of the coin: time expansion. Let's say you're a business executive and you have before you a twenty-page typewritten report which you must digest before entering a meeting. You would like to spend an hour at it, but have just fifteen minutes in which to thoroughly familiarize yourself with the material. You begin with a syllogism:

"For my effective presentation at the meeting, to view this reading as requiring an hour of my time is self-damaging.

"I need an effective presentation in order to maintain my status in the company.

"To the degree that I wish to maintain my status, I'll get an hour's worth of value from the next fifteen minutes."

And into the imagery. You see yourself, on the screen, scanning the material and just gobbling it up. As your eyes fly down the page, your mind catches and stores every point. You have worlds of time. The fifteen minutes seem to stretch out into a full hour. You glance at a clock on the wall, and the second hand appears to be scarcely moving. Back to your material. When you read the final line of the manuscript you look up to see that only fourteen minutes have passed since you started, and you remark to yourself, "I had plenty of time."

Before emerging, you give yourself a posthypnotic suggestion that your whole thinking mechanism will speed up so that the fifteen minutes available to you will be ample, as if it were a full hour.

Or, consider that you're about to go onto the concert stage to play a twenty-minute oboe solo, and you want to rehearse it in your mind. "But I have only four minutes before I go onstage," you say to yourself. "How can I do it?" Let us remember that a two-minute dream can span what seems like many hours. Surely you've dreamed of an hour-long climb up a mountain. If scientists in a sleep laboratory were to count the rapid eye movements that indicate when the dream started and ended, they could tell you it took two minutes. Similarly, the mental rehearsal of the twenty-minute oboe sonata—or anything else—can be completed in four minutes.

You picture it happening so on the screen. The piece flows through your mind, fully and effortlessly. You then suggest to yourself posthypnotically that the concentration of your faculties will be such that you will have the ability to rehearse mentally the entire twenty-minute sonata in just a few actual minutes. And you emerge from the raised state.

Such an approach, of course, lends itself to any situation where time is limited—for example, if you have more studying to do than the time available would seem to accommodate. Others have done it. So can you.

CHAPTER 12

The Critical Component

And there you have it—virtually everything I know about the practice of self-hypnosis. I'm being neither facetious nor falsely modest in saying so, for—as you have learned in this book—complex as the state itself may be to define or to fathom, the technique of achieving it and using it for self-therapy is remarkably simple.

This three-pronged weapon of *syllogism–self-imagery–posthypnotic* suggestion offers you the swiftest therapy to effect changes in mind and body that I know of, and all without outside help. In fact, there's even clinical evidence that you get better results without assistance from others. Dr. John Clifford Ruch conducted experiments in both self-hypnosis and heterohypnosis (hypnotic state induced by a second person) at Stanford University a few years ago. Summing up his findings, he wrote:

". . . Self-hypnosis without prior heterohypnosis is fully as effective as heterohypnosis. It is thus clear that the lore is incorrect. Subjects can obviously hypnotize themselves without prior training. . . . Furthermore, conventional hypnotic procedures do tend to inhibit self-hypnosis, rather than to create or even to help it, as is usually stated. On the contrary, initial self-hypnosis tends to help later heterohypnosis."

That is why I urge you to study the self-hypnotic procedure and practice it until you feel comfortable and proficient in inducing the relaxed state. Then use it in self-therapy for a reasonable length of time to see whether you get the results you seek. Only after experiencing negative results from such a fair trial should you scrap the technique or seek assistance from a specialist.

Obviously "a reasonable length of time" and "a fair trial" must necessarily be arbitrary and will differ from individual to individual, depending on such variables as susceptibility to hypnosis, diligence in practicing the exercise, the degree of involvement in the raised state and the depth of the problem or difficulty being treated.

Having set forth these variables, I offer the following rule of thumb: if, after three weeks of engaging in the exercise faithfully several times a day, giving each performance your full concentration and commitment, you still fail to see any signs that you may be moving in the direction of your designated goal, then you may fairly assume either that you're doing something wrong or that your symptom is so firmly anchored in emotional causes that you need professional aid in resolving it.

If such is the case, I would advise you first to reexamine every aspect of your self-hypnotic technique to try to find where you may be off the track, then, if you still fail to find an answer, seek outside help, either from a hypnotherapist or, if you sense a more soul-digging method may be in order, an expert in deeper therapy. Psychoanalysis is my preference, but as an analyst I just might be prejudiced.

This may sound oversimplified, but I conduct a practice in psychoanalysis, I teach self-hypnosis and I use it myself, all based on the single principle that we have a choice: we can either drift through our days, helplessly turning with whatever external wind may propel us, or we can elect to become masters of our own lives. I'm not talking about creating supermen, but within certain reasonable and practical limits we *can* gain control. I'm absolutely convinced of that. Perhaps the time has now come in your life to take charge where charge is possible.

You can expect to become faster and more adept at inducing

the hypnotic state with each performance of the exercise. In addition, you may also include an appropriate suggestion as a posthypnotic implant, namely:

"I'll find my skill in self-hypnotherapy increasing daily."

Thus, the advances that come through repetition of the exercise itself are strengthened by positive implants designed to reach the unconscious. With increased skill will come achievement, and from achievement self-confidence will grow—one will fuel the other, till you feel an inner strength that exceeds anything you have ever felt before. You can make that happen. This is not to claim that self-hypnosis is a cure-all. There's no magic in it; what it does is speed up results that could be achieved by more cumbersome methods of mental and emotional treatment.

The thesis of this book has clearly been to gain self-mastery through self-hypnosis. Before closing, let me mention a second major use of hypnosis as practiced in therapeutic settings: "uncovering"—that is, exploring the unconscious to discover what lies hidden in the labyrinths of one's memory. To uncover significant early experiences in our lives by hypnosis can be most useful. For example, hypnosis illuminated the key memory that led to the successful treatment of Fred, described in Chapter 9. Though psychic probing is usually accomplished under the direction of a second person, a psychotherapist or hypnotist, I would not discourage experimenting to unravel memory during self-hypnosis. Such information could prove valuable in your own self-treatment.

This uncovering aspect of hypnosis is also increasingly being tapped to help solve mysteries of a very practical nature. For instance, a person involved in an automobile accident may, through hypnosis, reach into his unconscious for critical details that had been forgotten. Noteworthy is the case of the kidnapping of twenty-six children in a bus at Chowchilla, California, in 1976. Under hypnosis, the bus driver was able to remember the license number of the kidnappers' van. This fascinating facet of hypnosis, the uncovering of memory, merits fuller exploration at another time.

For now, I am content to offer you this technique, so simple and easily learned, yet so powerful, that will have you feeling better about yourself. I encourage you to make a very personal matter of your self-mastery, with the emphasis on *self*. Emphasize feelings and emotions in your self-hypnosis. Their importance in mental and physical health is agreed on by therapists of every persuasion. That is why, in the self-hypnotic exercise, you visualize a tranquil spot where you feel at peace, imagine caring for your body and mind as tenderly as you would a loved one, and sketch a mental picture of yourself as you would like to be—and can be. That is also why, after learning the technique, you are advised to change the wording and imagery to make it uniquely your own.

So ends my advice. This book and I, like any teacher, can lead you just so far. I can set you on the path and point the direction, but you, equipped with the mental tools and confidence for the journey, must travel alone.

Such is the aim of analysis: to build the ego-strength that will enable the individual to function productively and happily. So let it be with self-hypnosis, in which the most critical component is the perpendicular pronoun: I.

BIBLIOGRAPHY

AUGUST, R. V. *Hypnosis in Obstetrics*. New York: McGraw-Hill (Blakiston), 1961.

BARBER, THEODORE X., ed. *Advances in Altered States of Consciousness & Human Potentialities*, Vol. I. New York: Psychological Dimensions, Inc., 1976.

BENSON, HERBERT. *The Relaxation Response*. New York: William Morrow and Company, Inc., 1975.

BERGLER, EDMUND. *Selected Papers of Edmund Bergler, M.D.* New York: Grune & Stratton, Inc., 1969.

——. "The Use and Misuse of Analytic Interpretations by the Patient." *The Psychoanalytic Review*, Vol. 33, No. 4, October 1946.

BERNHARDT, ROGER. *Personality Characteristics of Stutterers*. Unpublished doctoral dissertation, University of Michigan, 1953.

BLYTHE, PETER. *Hypnotism: Its Power and Practice*. New York: Taplinger Publishing Co., Inc., 1971.

"Can Your Patients Benefit from Hypnotherapy?" *Patient Care*, December 1, 1973, pp. 22–23.

CAPRIO, FRANK S., and JOSEPH R. BERGER. *Helping Yourself with Self-Hypnosis*. New York: Warner Paperback Library, 1972.

CAUTELA, JOSEPH R. "The Use of Court Conditioning in Hypnotherapy." *The International Journal of Clinical and Experimental Hypnosis*, Vol. XXIII, No. 1, January 1975, pp. 15–27.

CLARK, MICHAEL. "Hypnosis—An Alternative to Pill-Popping for Severe Pain." *Prevention*, July 1976, pp. 61–65.

ERICKSON, MILTON H. (Jay Haley, ed.) *Advanced Techniques of Hypnosis and Therapy*. New York and London: Grune & Stratton, Inc., 1967.

ESTABROOKS, GEORGE H. *Hypnotism*. New York: E. P. Dutton & Co., Inc., 1957.

FREUD, SIGMUND. "The Unconscious (1915)." *Collected Papers*, Vol. 4, pp. 98–136, London: The Hogarth Press, 1949.

——. "Hypnotism and Suggestion (1888)." *Collected Papers*, Vol. 5, pp. 11–24, London: The Hogarth Press, 1950.

FROMM, ERIKA, and RONALD E. SHOR, eds. *HYPNOSIS: Research Developments and Perspectives*. Chicago and New York: Aldine-Atherton, Inc., 1972.

GIANNITRAPANI, CORINNE, with DORIS GRUENWALD. "An Experience in Autohypnosis." *The International Journal of Clinical and Experimental Hypnosis,* Vol. XXII, No. 1, January 1974, pp. 1–8.

HERRON, WILLIAM G. "The Evidence for the Unconscious." *Psychoanalysis and the Psychoanalytic Review,* Vol. 49, No. 1, Spring 1962, pp. 70–92.

HILGARD, ERNEST R. *The Experience of Hypnosis.* New York: Harcourt, Brace & World, Inc., 1968.

———. "Hypnosis Is No Mirage." *Psychology Today,* November 1974, pp. 121–128.

HILGARD, JOSEPHINE R. "Imaginative Involvement: Some Characteristics of the Highly Hypnotizable and the Non-Hypnotizable." *The International Journal of Clinical and Experimental Hypnosis,* Vol. XXII, No. 2, April 1974, pp. 138–156.

HULL, CLARK L. *Hypnosis and Suggestibility.* New York: Appleton-Century, 1933.

HUSSAIN, A. "Behavior Therapy Using Hypnosis." *The Conditioning Therapies: The Challenge in Psychotherapy.* Joseph Wolpe and others, eds. New York: Holt, Rinehart and Winston, Inc., 1964.

"Hypnosis." *Encyclopaedia Britannica,* 1969, Vol. 11, pp. 995–997.

JACOBSON, EDMUND. *You Must Relax.* New York: McGraw-Hill Book Company, Inc., 1962.

JAMPOLSKY, GERALD G., and GAYL WESTERMAN. *A Unique Suggestive and Auto Suggestive Technique to Help Children with Reading Problems.* Kentfield, California: The Child Center, 1973.

LECRON, LESLIE M. *The Complete Guide to Hypnosis.* New York: Barnes & Noble Books, 1973.

———. *Self Hypnotism.* New York: The New American Library, Inc., 1970.

MCBRAYER, JAMES T. *The Key to Hypnotism Simplified.* New York: Bell Publishing Company, 1962.

MARCUSE, F. L. *Hypnosis—Fact and Fiction.* Baltimore: Penguin Books, 1959.

MILLER, ROBERT J. "Response to the Ponzo Illusion as a Reflection of Hypnotic Susceptibility." *The International Journal of Clinical and Experimental Hypnosis,* Vol. XXIII, No. 2, April 1975, pp. 148–157.

MORGAN, ARLENE H., DAVID L. JOHNSON, and ERNEST R. HILGARD. "The Stability of Hypnotic Susceptibility: A Longitudinal

Study." *The International Journal of Clinical and Experimental Hypnosis,* Vol. XXII, No. 3, July 1974, pp. 249–257.

OUSBY, W. J. *Self-Hypnosis & Scientific Self-Suggestion.* London: Thursons Publishers, Ltd., 1966.

——. *The Theory and Practice of Hypnotism.* New York: Arco Publishing Company, Inc., 1973.

PEALE, NORMAN VINCENT. *The Power of Positive Thinking.* Greenwich, Connecticut: Fawcett Publications, Inc., 1956.

PULVER, SYDNEY E. and MITCHELL P. "Hypnosis in Medical and Dental Practice: A Survey." *The International Journal of Clinical and Experimental Hypnosis,* Vol. XXIII, No. 1, January 1975, pp. 28–47.

RHODES, RAPHAEL H. *Hypnosis: Theory, Practice and Application.* New York: Gramercy Publishing Co., 1950.

RIEGEL, MICHELLE GALLER. "Pain Control Through Hypnosis." *Science News,* Vol. 110, No. 18, October 30, 1976, pp. 283–285.

ROSEN, HAROLD. "Hypnosis." *Encyclopedia Americana,* 1976, Vol. 14, pp. 679–682.

RUCH, JOHN CLIFFORD. *A Study of Self-Hypnosis under Alternative Procedures.* Unpublished doctoral dissertation, Stanford University, 1972.

SALTER, ANDREW. *What Is Hypnosis.* New York: Farrar, Straus and Giroux, 1973.

SCHWARTZ, HERMAN S. *The Art of Relaxation.* Elmhurst, New York: Sessions Publishers, 1959.

SELLERS, DAVID J. "Teaching a Self-Initiated Control Technique to Individuals and a Group in College." *The International Journal of Clinical and Experimental Hypnosis,* Vol. XXII, No. 1, January 1974, pp. 39–45.

SPIEGEL, HERBERT. "Current Perspectives on Hypnosis in Obstetrics." *Acta Psychotherapeutica,* Vol. II, No. 6, 1963, pp. 412–429.

——. "An Eye-Roll Test for Hypnotizability." *The American Journal of Clinical Hypnosis,* Vol. 15, No. 1, July 1972, pp. 25–28.

——. "Hypnosis and the Psychotherapeutic Process." *Comprehensive Psychiatry,* Vol. I, No. 3, June 1960, pp. 174–185.

——. "Is Symptom Removal Dangerous?" *The American Journal of Psychiatry,* Vol. 123, No. 10, April 1967, pp. 1279–1283.

——. *Manual for Hypnotic Induction Profile.* New York: Soni Medica, Inc., 1970.

——. "A Single-Treatment Method to Stop Smoking Using Ancillary

Self-Hypnosis." *The International Journal of Clinical and Experimental Hypnosis,* Vol. XVIII, No. 4, 1970, pp. 235–267.

——, and LOUIS LINN. "The 'Ripple Effect' Following Adjunct Hypnosis in Analytic Psychotherapy." *The American Journal of Psychiatry,* Vol. 126, No. 1, July 1969, pp. 91–96.

SUINN, RICHARD M. "Body Thinking: Psychology for Olympic Champs." *Psychology Today,* July 1976, pp. 38–43.

VAN NUYS, DAVID. "Meditation, Attention, and Hypnotic Susceptibility: A Correlational Study." *The International Journal of Clinical and Experimental Hypnosis,* Vol. XXI, No. 2, April 1973, pp. 56–69.

WEITZENHOFFER, ANDRÉ M., and ERNEST R. HILGARD. *Stanford Hypnotic Susceptibility Scale.* Palo Alto, California: Consulting Psychologists Press, Inc., 1959.

WOLBERG, LEWIS R. *HYPNOSIS: Is It for You?* New York: Harcourt Brace Jovanovich, Inc., 1972.

——. *Medical Hypnosis.* New York: Grune & Stratton, 1948.

Index